Privacy and Confidentiality Issues

A Guide for Libraries and Their Lawyers

Theresa Chmara

American Library Association
Chicago 2009

Theresa Chmara is a partner in the Washington, D.C., office of Jenner and Block. She is a 1985 cum laude graduate of Boston College and a 1988 cum laude graduate of Georgetown University Law Center. While at Jenner and Block, she has been a trial and appellate litigator working on matters involving advertising, antitrust, administrative, constitutional, and First Amendment issues. Chmara has represented the American Library Association, the Freedom to Read Foundation, and the American Booksellers Association on free speech issues, and she has participated in matters before the U.S. Supreme Court and numerous other federal and state courts related to First Amendment issues. She has also participated as a faculty member at several Lawyers for Libraries training institutes designed to train attorneys to handle First Amendment issues for libraries.

While extensive effort has gone into ensuring the reliability of information appearing in this book, the publisher makes no warranty, express or implied, on the accuracy or reliability of the information, and does not assume and hereby disclaims any liability to any person for any loss or damage caused by errors or omissions in this publication.

The paper used in this publication meets the minimum requirements of American National Standard for Information Sciences—Permanence of Paper for Printed Library Materials, ANSI Z39.48-1992. ∞

Library of Congress Cataloging-in-Publication Data

Chmara, Theresa.
  Privacy and confidentiality issues : a guide for libraries and their lawyers / Theresa Chmara.
    p. cm.
  Includes bibliographical references and index.
  ISBN 978-0-8389-0970-6 (alk. paper)
  1. Library legislation—United States. 2. Library legislation—United States—States. 3. Privacy, Right of—United States. 4. Confidential communications—Library records—United States. I. Title.
  KF4315.C47 2009
  344.73'092—dc22

                                                                                        2008034902

ISBN-13: 978-0-8389-0970-6

Printed in the United States of America
13 12 11 10 09   5 4 3 2 1

Contents

Chapter One

WHEN DO PRIVACY AND CONFIDENTIALITY ISSUES ARISE?

It is a typical afternoon in the Main Street Public Library. A group of elementary-school-age children is enthralled by a librarian reading a book in the children's room. A group of business people gather in the meeting room for a discussion of zoning issues. The local historical association works on an exhibit for the display case that they may utilize until the end of the month. A group of high school teenagers desperately asks a research librarian for assistance in gathering information on the American Revolutionary War for a term paper due the next day. In the periodical room, an elderly patron asks the librarian for assistance in finding an article that a friend mentioned contained useful information about arthritis. The telephone rings; a patron needs assistance tracking down a consumer magazine that rates dishwashers. These patrons are exercising their First Amendment right to receive information, speak, and associate with the assistance of library staff.

Other patrons read and peruse books, periodicals, or information on the Internet without the assistance of the library staff—exercising their First Amendment right to receive information in a quiet, personal manner. A young girl, too shy to ask for assistance, is trying to find information on the Internet about breast cancer because she was just told by her mother that a favorite aunt had been diagnosed with the disease. A young man quietly reviews a book on alcoholism, an issue that has touched his own family. A middle-aged couple searches for information on teenage pregnancy, having just learned that their daughter is pregnant. An elderly man—feeling forgetful lately and concerned about what is happening to him—selects a book on Alzheimer's disease. The line at the desk lengthens as patrons make their book selections. The library is bustling. The community is using the library to learn, study, and enjoy books and other sources of information. Some patrons use the assistance of the library staff to find sources of interest; others use the library to gather information on sensitive topics that they prefer not to discuss with family, friends, or library staff. In each case the library serves as a critical link for patrons in the community to information they need but might otherwise not be able to access. In each case the patron exercises his or her First Amendment right to receive information.

That same afternoon, a sheriff comes to the Main Street Public Library with a subpoena. The subpoena requires the library staff to provide information about patron borrowing records. Specifically, the subpoena requires the library staff to provide the names and addresses of patrons who have borrowed books on childbearing in the last nine months. Absurd and impossible, most people would say when presented with this scenario. It is not impossible. This is a subpoena request that a librarian actually received several years ago.

The sheriff's office was investigating a child abandonment case and believed that the person who had abandoned the child *may* have borrowed a book on childbearing from the library to enable her to birth the baby on her own prior to abandoning the child. The law enforcement officers had a legitimate investigation on their hands. It was, however, pure speculation that the person who abandoned the child had borrowed any books from the library to facilitate the criminal act. How did the library react? How should a library react in the same situation?

The library that received the request for information on patrons borrowing books on childbearing had a confidentiality policy that protected patron records. The librarian was appalled at the prospect that patron records would be produced and patrons then questioned about the library books they had borrowed. One can imagine the horror a patron might feel at having a sheriff's officer show up on her doorstep asking her why she had borrowed books on childbearing. Perhaps a teenage girl learned she was pregnant and had borrowed books to prepare her for the pregnancy. She may have failed to inform her family of her predicament, but she certainly had committed no crime. Perhaps our middle-aged couple from the Main Street Public Library had borrowed some books on childbearing to share with their own teenage daughter about her pregnancy. When they did so, they certainly did not intend to share the knowledge of their daughter's pregnancy with strangers. Must the library produce this information about its patrons' reading choices? Must the patrons provide explanations for why they are borrowing certain books?

What should a librarian do when faced with such a demand? The particular librarian who received the request for the names of patrons borrowing books on childbearing immediately (and wisely) called her city attorney. She feared that if the library were put in the position of divulging the reading habits of its patrons, members of the community would be chilled in the exercise of their First Amendment rights. She was concerned that if the community learned that the library had responded to a request for patron circulation records without any objection, many patrons would decide not to borrow sensitive material from the library. Of course, for many patrons of limited financial resources, the library is the only place where they can go to secure such information. Library staff should immediately contact legal counsel if a request for patron use or circulation information is received.

What should the attorney do? Must the attorney advise the librarian to provide the patron information? Is there any recourse for the attorney to protect the First Amendment rights of the library or library patrons? What rights exactly do patrons have to preserve the confidentiality of their borrowing records? These are the questions that will be explored and discussed in the chapters ahead.

Criminal investigations are not the only instances that prompt requests to libraries for patron information. A request for patron information can be generated as a Freedom of Information Act or an Open Records Act request. Most states allow citizens to request information from a public institution such as a library. Many states, however, exempt personally identifying information, and some specifically exempt patron use information in libraries.

Several years ago, an employer learned that several employees were using Internet connections through the public library to access sites for which the employer was being charged thousands of dollars in long-distance communications. Of course, the employer also sustained the cost of many hours of lost employment caused by the workers' using business hours for personal pursuits. There is no doubt that the employer had a legitimate interest in identifying the employees. The employer commenced an investigation and could pinpoint the time that the employees made the calls. The employer deciphered the identification numbers used by the employees to access the library system. But the employer could not discover the identities of the employees. The employer filed an Open Records Act request with the library and asked it to provide the names and addresses of the patrons whose identification numbers were supplied. The library faced with this request similarly turned to its attorney for advice, and litigation ensued when the library refused to release the names of its patrons. Once again, the issue boiled down to whether a legitimate need for information outweighed the critical First Amendment rights of patrons.

This book will explore the various issues connected with requests for patron circulation records or library use records and the First Amendment rights at stake when libraries are asked to produce those records. The book will discuss these issues with respect to both circulation records and Internet use records. Additionally, the book will analyze the role of the library as employer with respect to hostile work environment issues and the confidentiality issues that arise in that area. Finally, the book will provide practical advice to librarians and their lawyers in drafting privacy and confidentiality policies that provide the maximum First Amendment protection for library patrons.

Chapter Two

THE FIRST AMENDMENT AND OTHER LEGAL CONSIDERATIONS

This chapter focuses on three general issues: (1) the need for privacy policies protecting the privacy rights of patrons; (2) the types of policies that a library should adopt; and (3) the appropriate response when a request for patron information has been made that would involve disclosing information protected by the library's privacy policy. Legal counsel should be consulted to assist with drafting library privacy policies and responding to requests for information that would violate the privacy policy.

What are the First Amendment rights that exist in the library context?

The First Amendment generally protects citizens from governmental restrictions that place a burden on the right to speak or the right to receive information. In the library context, it is the right to receive information that must be protected. Governmental restrictions implicating First Amendment rights are unconstitutional if they place an outright ban on receiving information or impermissibly burden the ability of a person to receive information.

Is privacy explicitly protected by the First Amendment?

No. The First Amendment rights of patrons are violated, however, when the release of patron information causes patrons to be chilled in the exercise of their free speech rights. First Amendment rights are implicated if patrons are inhibited from choosing library materials because their reading choices might be revealed publicly.

Why should a library have a policy of protecting the privacy rights of its patrons?

When patrons use the library, they expect that library personnel will make every possible effort to protect their privacy. Patrons expect that the books they choose to read, the materials they select to borrow, the Internet sites they visit, and the resources they utilize while in the library will not be divulged publicly. In making those choices to read and receive information, patrons are exercising their First Amendment rights. If privacy is not maintained by the library, patrons will be chilled in the exercise of their First Amendment rights. Patrons will refrain from selecting certain reading materials, fearing public disclosure. Patrons specifically will avoid materials that are considered controversial or sensitive, fearing that their particular reading choices could subject them to interrogation, public ridicule, or embarrassment.

What type of policy should the library adopt?

Libraries should consult with legal counsel when drafting a privacy policy. In general, the policy should state that it protects the privacy and First Amendment rights of its patrons. The policy should state further that the library will not release any personally identifying information about a particular patron's use of library materials and resources without the explicit permission of the patron or an order of the court demanding release of the information. With the increased availability of library materials other than books, the library should ensure that its privacy and confidentiality policy includes patron use information related to other materials. A privacy policy should include patron use information related to books, videos, audiotapes, and the Internet. As the library expands the availability of its information sources, it must ensure that its policy evolves to include the many ways that the community utilizes the resources in the library.

Where should the policy appear?

The library privacy and confidentiality policy should be posted in the library. Patrons should be aware that their selection and use of reading and other library materials will be protected from public disclosure and scrutiny. As with other library policies, a policy regarding privacy and confidentiality should be posted at the circulation desk, next to Internet terminals, and at other critical areas of the library to maximize community awareness of the protections afforded to patrons by the library. New patrons should be directed to library policies at the time they receive a library card or otherwise register as library users.

What kind of data collection would such a policy allow?

The privacy and confidentiality policy would not preclude the library from gathering and releasing *general* statistical information about the use of library materials by patrons. For example, the library could compile and release information about the number of patrons utilizing the library's materials and their collective borrowing habits. Thus, if a public interest would be served, the library could release the information that 200 people borrowed materials related to the subject of abortion or AIDS but could not release the names of the specific people who had borrowed those particular books. The release of general information about patron borrowing might be useful to the public and the library board in determining the interests of the community. No useful purpose is served, however, in disclosing that John Doe borrowed a book on AIDS or Jane Doe borrowed a book on abortion. In fact, when John and Jane borrowed those books from the library it was certainly with the expectation that their reading choices would not be revealed to the public.

Which staff members should know about the policy?

The library must train all librarians and other personnel concerning the privacy and confidentiality policy maintained by the library. The policy will be worthless if staff are not aware of the policy and prepared to address requests from the public for patron use information. It is critical that *all* library staff with access to patron use information receive training as to the policy itself and the reasons behind the adoption of the policy. An informed staff will be equipped to address important privacy concerns on a daily basis. Staff should also be informed about any laws in a particular state that prohibit or exempt the disclosure of patron use information. Procedures should be established for staff confronted by a request for information. Often, a request for information (particularly if informal) will be directed to library staff at the circulation desk. Thus, all library staff must be trained.

What should the library do when a request is made for patron use information?

As will be discussed in greater detail below, the appropriate response will depend largely on the type of request being made, the requester, and the specific federal or state laws relating to the particular request for information. There are six potential scenarios: (1) an informal request for information from a federal, state, or local law enforcement official, or from a private litigant, citizen, parent, or spouse; (2) an Open Records Act request for information from a citizen or member of the media; (3) a subpoena request for information from a federal, state, or local law enforcement official or from a private attorney involved in a civil suit; (4) a search warrant demand from a federal, state, or local law enforcement official; (5) a Patriot Act request from a federal law enforcement official; or (6) a National Security Letter request from a federal law enforcement official. Regardless of the type of request made, the library should take all possible steps to protect the privacy and First Amendment interests of its patrons.

What should the library do if it receives an informal request for patron information?

An informal request could come from a parent, spouse, law enforcement officer, or journalist. The library staff person receiving the request should inform the requester that library policy prohibits the release of personally identifying information about particular patrons. The requester should be shown the policy and any explanations supporting the policy. In many states (as will be discussed in greater detail in chapter 4), specific legislation exempts or prohibits a library from releasing patron use information without the explicit permission of the patron, a court order, or a subpoena. The requester should be informed of any legislation that bars the request.

Do different rules apply to videos?

A federal law called the Video Privacy Protection Act (also discussed in chapter 6) explicitly prohibits the release of information related to video use. This federal legislation applies in every state. This legislation was enacted in 1988 in response to a public uproar after the video rental records of a U.S. Supreme Court nominee were publicly released during that individual's Senate confirmation hearings. Judge Robert Bork was nominated to the U.S. Supreme Court. During his hearings, his video rental records were released. After a public outcry that such information should be private and confidential, the U.S. Congress enacted legislation prohibiting such public disclosures. With the increased availability of videos in library collections, library staff training should emphasize that privacy protection for patron use information extends to video and audio materials.

What should the library do if it receives an Open Records Act request or a Freedom of Information Act request?

Because a public library is a government institution, it may receive an Open Records or Freedom of Information Act request for patron use information. Virtually every state (see chapter 4) exempts libraries or affirmatively prohibits libraries from disclosing library circulation records or information related to the use of library materials by particular patrons. The exemption may not apply if the request is for general or aggregate information, the disclosure of which will not reveal information about a particular patron's use of library materials. If a library receives this type of request, it should consult with legal counsel to ensure that the appropriate response is provided to the requester pursuant to state or local laws governing such requests.

What should the library do if it receives a subpoena request for information?

The library should consult legal counsel immediately. A subpoena is not a court order. It cannot, however, be ignored. Legal procedures governing subpoenas may vary from jurisdiction to jurisdiction and court to court. A request for information pursuant to a subpoena may require some type of formal response. A subpoena can be issued by a law enforcement officer or an attorney in a civil case. If disclosure of the requested information would violate the library's privacy policy, legal counsel will assist the library in determining the appropriate method by which to object.

Can a library discuss the subpoena with anyone other than legal counsel?

A subpoena may require or request that the recipient not divulge the request itself or the contents of the request. The library should ask legal counsel to review the subpoena and ascertain whether there are any requirements to refrain from discussing the subpoena. Requests from law enforcement personnel will often contain a "gag order" requesting nondisclosure.

What should the library attorney do if the library has received a subpoena request for information from an attorney in a civil proceeding in which the library is not a party?

In a civil case (a court case between two private parties, as opposed to a criminal matter), court rules may permit the library to merely send the requesting attorney a letter objecting to the subpoena. If an objection letter is permitted, then the library will be spared the expense and time needed to file its own motion with the court requesting relief from any obligation to produce patron use information. The onus would then be on the requesting party and its attorney to file a motion with the court to compel the production of the information. If such a motion to compel production is filed, the library will have the opportunity to argue in the court proceeding that the private information should not be produced.

What should the library attorney do if the library receives a subpoena request for information from a law enforcement officer?

In the first instance, the library attorney should make contact with the law enforcement officer (often a prosecutor) to explain why the library objects to the production of patron use information in the absence of a court order. Often the law enforcement officer has not focused on the First Amendment implications of the request for patron use information and has not anticipated the possibility of a court battle over the subpoena request. An informal discussion will permit law enforcement personnel to assess their need for the requested information, the First Amendment issues involved, and the potential impact on their investigation of a protracted legal battle over whether the information should be disclosed. An assessment of the First Amendment issues might persuade the law enforcement officer to withdraw the subpoena.

What should the library attorney do if a law enforcement officer refuses to withdraw a subpoena request for information?

If law enforcement personnel will not withdraw a subpoena request, a library attorney should file a motion to quash the subpoena. If the court orders the subpoena "quashed," then the library will not be under an obligation to produce any information. The motion should outline the First Amendment issues at stake and urge the court to quash the subpoena unless the requesting party can demonstrate in court that there is a compelling need for the information, a reasonable nexus between the request and the information sought, and no reasonable alternative way to gather the information.

Why should the library and its counsel object to subpoena requests?

Often a subpoena is a fishing expedition. Without any real *need* for the information (as opposed to interest in the information) or basis to believe that the information will lead to the solution of a crime or the resolution of a legal issue, someone requests patron use information through the use of a subpoena. The library cannot determine from the face of a subpoena whether the requester has a legitimate, compelling need for the information and whether a nexus between the requested information and the purported need exists. The library does, however, have an obligation to protect the privacy and First Amendment rights of its patrons. A court will balance the interests of both sides. Recognizing the critical importance of the First Amendment, courts require the requester (often a law enforcement official) to demonstrate a compelling need for the information, a nexus between the request and the investigation, and that no reasonable alternative means exists to gather the information.

What should a library do if a law enforcement officer produces a search warrant for information?

In contrast to a subpoena request, a search warrant necessitates a search by law enforcement for particular information in the library rather than a search by the library in response to a subpoena request. A search warrant is, by definition, more intrusive in that law enforcement will need virtually free access to the library and its files and computers—limited only by the description of records to be searched in the warrant. During the course of a search warrant execution, law enforcement officials will have access to a broad range of information concerning patrons that will necessarily impact the rights of patrons who have nothing whatsoever to do with any criminal investigation. Nonetheless, because a search warrant is issued by a court and generally requires immediate execution by the law enforcement personnel, the library may have no recourse but to permit the search to take place.

Can the library do anything to stop law enforcement from executing a search warrant?

A library can request that a law enforcement officer refrain from executing a search warrant, but it should not refuse access to the law enforcement officer if the request is denied. Although approved by a court, a search warrant often is secured by law enforcement without allowing the court to consider the First Amendment implications of the disclosure of patron use information. In approving the warrant, the court hears only from the law enforcement officers, who are unlikely to highlight any First Amendment issues. Thus, if a law enforcement officer arrives at the library with a search warrant that will require searching for or reviewing information related to patron circulation or use records, library staff should ask for an opportunity to contact legal counsel. Legal counsel may be able to persuade the law enforcement personnel to allow the courts to conduct the balancing of interests that often is conducted in the subpoena process. If library staff are not the target of an investigation (and thus there is no fear that evidence will be destroyed), the police officers may be willing to wait a few days to allow library legal counsel to raise the First Amendment concerns. See the Tattered Cover case study below.

CASE STUDY: TATTERED COVER

Law enforcement discovered a methamphetamine lab in a home in which several individuals lived. They also found several books on how to make methamphetamines and a discarded invoice in the trash from the Tattered Cover bookstore that listed the customer's name, but not the titles of the books purchased. Law enforcement officials believed that the person who had purchased the books necessarily was the person who had built the lab.

The Tattered Cover bookstore in Denver was presented with a sub- poena for information about a customer's book purchases for a one-

(cont.)

---

month period. The bookstore resisted on the ground that disclosure of the information would implicate the privacy and First Amendment interests of its customers. Law enforcement officials then applied for a search warrant. Five police officers proceeded to the store to search customer records. The owner of the bookstore, with the assistance of legal counsel, persuaded them to wait five days before executing the search warrant. Counsel then filed a lawsuit requesting that the court enjoin the officers from executing the search warrant.

Tattered Cover was supported by many organizations in an amicus capacity. Groups such as the American Library Association, the Freedom to Read Foundation, and the American Booksellers Foundation for Free Expression argued that it would set a dangerous precedent to assume that the commission of a crime (the construction of a methamphetamine lab) could be proven by showing who had purchased certain books (books related to methamphetamine manufacture and drug laboratory construction). Simply reading a book is not a crime.

The Colorado Supreme Court agreed. In *Tattered Cover, Inc. v. The City of Thornton,* 44 P.3d 1044 (Colo. 2002), the court held that the government had failed to "demonstrate that its need for this evidence is sufficiently compelling to outweigh the harmful effects of the search warrant." The court held that "both the First Amendment to the United States Constitution and Article II, Section 10 of the Colorado Constitution protect an individual's fundamental right to purchase books anonymously, free from governmental interference" and that "law enforcement officials implicate this right when they seek judicial approval of a search warrant authorizing seizure of customer purchase records from an innocent, third-party bookseller."

Can library staff demand that legal counsel be present during the execution of a search warrant?

Even if law enforcement officers will not concede to a wait that would allow a legal challenge to the search warrant by the library, they should be urged to await the arrival of legal counsel for the search itself. An attorney should be present to review the search warrant, ensure its legality, and monitor the search itself to ensure that the law enforcement personnel are following the warrant exactly. Library personnel and library counsel should also monitor the search. Because search warrants are approved by the court, they will be very specific and definite in their terms. Thus, the warrant may permit a search of computer records alone or, even more specifically, a search of a particular computer. In that case, the library staff and counsel should direct the law enforcement officers to the location of such records rather than permitting them unfettered access to the entire library. Similarly, if the search warrant only permits a search for the records of one patron, the library staff and counsel should assist the law enforcement officers in locating those records alone rather than permitting them access to *all* patron records. If the library cannot forestall a search by warrant through a court challenge, it should strive nonetheless to ensure the greatest protection of its patron use information during the execution of the search by providing access only to those items specifically itemized in the search warrant.

Can a library discuss a search warrant with anyone other than legal counsel?

A search warrant may require that the recipient not divulge the request itself or the contents of the request. The library should ask legal counsel to review the text of the search warrant and ascertain whether there are any requirements to refrain from discussing it during the search itself or once the search by law enforcement has been completed. Search warrants directed to third parties that are not the actual subjects of the investigation will often contain a "gag order" requesting nondisclosure if there is a concern that the actual subject of the investigation will flee or destroy evidence.

What should the library do if it receives a Section 215 Patriot Act request?

Library staff should immediately contact legal counsel if the library receives a request for information pursuant to Section 215 of the federal Patriot Act. Amendments to the Patriot Act in 2006 provide a mechanism for challenging a request for information. (A full explanation of the history, legal objections, and process for objecting to a Section 215 request can be found in chapter 6.) All Section 215 requests have a "gag order" that prohibits the recipient from disclosing the request to anyone other than legal counsel and a person that "needs" to know in order to facilitate a response to the request. (A full explanation of the gag order aspect of Patriot Act requests also can be found in chapter 6.)

What should the library do if it receives a National Security Letter request for patron use information?

As with a Patriot Act request, library staff should immediately contact legal counsel if the library receives a request for information pursuant to a National Security Letter (NSL). Amendments to the Patriot Act in 2006 provide a mechanism for challenging a request for information. (A full explanation of the history, legal objections, and process for objecting to a National Security Letter request can be found in chapter 6.) All NSL requests have a "gag order" that prohibits the recipient from disclosing the request to anyone other than legal counsel and any person that "needs" to know in order to facilitate a response to the request. (A full explanation of the gag order aspects of National Security Letters can be found in chapter 6.)

How should legal counsel prepare a case to either defend against a motion to compel or support a motion to quash?

Before a librarian or library attorney can analyze whether responding to a request for patron use information violates the First Amendment, he or she must determine what First Amendment protections apply in such a context. A determination of whether the library is a public forum and whether there is a First Amendment right to receive information in the library are critical first steps in that analysis.

What is a public forum?

The determination of whether the First Amendment protects expressive activity in a particular context depends in the first instance on a determination of whether the location where the expressive activity is taking place is a public forum. Government property is categorized in one of three different ways: (1) a traditional public forum, (2) a designated or limited public forum, or (3) a nonpublic forum. A city sidewalk or city park is considered a quintessential or traditional public forum.

Is a library considered a public forum?

Courts repeatedly have found that libraries are considered a designated or limited public forum for the *receipt* of information, but not for the *expression* of information. A library certainly can prohibit a person from making speeches in the reading rooms, picketing, or otherwise expressing himself in the library in a manner that is disruptive to other patrons. The library has a justifiable interest in maintaining peace and order that will allow all patrons the quiet enjoyment of the library. The courts have held, however, that a library is a designated or limited public forum for the receipt of information. See the *Kreimer v. Morristown* case study below.

CASE STUDY: *KREIMER V. MORRISTOWN*

Richard Kreimer, a homeless man, was banned from the Morristown, New Jersey, library for disrupting patrons and because his personal hygiene was offensive to other patrons. The Third Circuit Court of Appeals held unequivocally that the First Amendment protects the right to *receive* information and "includes the right to some level of access to a public library, the quintessential locus of the receipt of information" (*Kreimer v. Bureau of Police for the Town of Morristown,* 958 F.2d 1242, 1255 [3d Cir. 1992]).

The appellate court emphasized, however, that a public library is a quintessential public forum for *access to information,* but *not* (unless specifically authorized by the library) for engaging in other types of expressive activities (such as making speeches, distributing pamphlets, etc.). The court found that the Morristown Library had "intentionally opened the Library to the public" for "specified purposes: reading, studying, using the Library materials" (*id.* at 1259–60). The court thus held that the library has the right to establish reasonable rules governing library use and that the library's power to regulate patron behavior is *not* limited to cases of "actual disruption."

The Third Circuit held specifically that libraries may regulate non-expressive activity designed to promote safety or efficient access to materials, such as rules requiring patrons to be engaged in library-associated activities, rules prohibiting harassment, and a rule that permitted librarians to remove patrons with offensive bodily hygiene that constitutes a nuisance to others. Importantly, the *Kreimer* case settled before the court had an opportunity to apply these general principles to the particular facts of the case and determine whether the Morristown rules were applied in a constitutional manner to Mr. Kreimer.

Does the First Amendment include a right to receive information?

That the First Amendment right to speak includes the corollary right to receive information is a well-established principle of First Amendment jurisprudence. The U.S. Supreme Court has held that the Constitution protects the right to receive information and ideas because this is a fundamental aspect of the rights of free speech. Thus, the right to *receive* information is a protected expressive activity under the First Amendment.

If a location is deemed a public forum or a designated public forum, can the entity impose any restrictions on First Amendment rights?

In either a public forum or a designated public forum, the government may only impose restrictions on the *content* of speech if it can demonstrate that the regulation is necessary to achieve a compelling state interest and has been narrowly drawn.[1] A *content-neutral* prohibition on speech is permitted if it is narrowly tailored to achieve a significant government interest and leaves open ample alternative channels of communication.[2] Thus, because a library likely will be considered a designated public forum for the receipt of information, any action by the government that prohibits speech or otherwise chills the exercise of First Amendment rights is a violation of the Constitution if it cannot meet these tests.

Can the library impose restrictions on use of the library that are unrelated to the content of the speech?

Yes. The library may impose content-neutral time, place, and manner restrictions that are reasonable and necessary. For example, the library can impose time limits on the use of Internet terminals or set a limit on the number of pages that can be printed without a fee. The library can set limits on how many books or videos can be borrowed and can set a length of time that materials may be retained. The library may require that reference materials remain in certain rooms of the library. Regulations of this type are content-neutral, necessary for the efficient operation of the library, and reasonable. Time, place, and manner restrictions do not impose an undue burden on the exercise of First Amendment rights.

Are patron use records privileged from disclosure?

There is very little case law directly on the subject. The Supreme Court has never considered the issue. However, the case law that exists from lower courts and state courts as well as analogous First Amendment cases decided by the Supreme Court strongly supports the position that a *qualified* privilege exists. The importance of the First Amendment rights at stake has resulted in courts applying a balancing test to determine whether the needs of the requester outweigh the free speech rights implicated by disclosure of the information. The Supreme Court has held that a person's constitutional rights are violated when she is prevented outright from exercising her First Amendment rights or when obstacles are placed in the way of the exercise of her First Amendment rights so as to chill her in the exercise of those rights.[3] The disclosure of library use records chills speech and places an undue burden on First Amendment rights. Thus, every request for information must be examined on its own facts to determine whether the information should be divulged. The requester should be put to the test to dissuade fishing expeditions and harassment. Requests for patron use information should be disclosed only if the requester can demonstrate a compelling need for the information, a reasonable likelihood that the information sought is relevant to a criminal investigation, and that there is no alternative means to secure the requested information.

What legal test is applied to determine whether a request for information should be denied on the basis of the First Amendment principles implicated?

The U.S. Supreme Court's decision in *Branzburg v. Hayes* is the starting point of any analysis in this area.[4] The Court consolidated three separate cases in which news reporters argued that they should not be compelled to respond to grand jury requests. In the case of Mr. Branzburg, he was asked directly to reveal a source. Branzburg had written two articles about the "drug scene" in Frankfort, Kentucky. The first article was accompanied by a picture of two hands making a drug called hashish; the second article contained interviews with drug users who apparently had smoked marijuana in the presence of Branzburg. The grand jury specifically requested the names of Branzburg's sources. After evaluating the facts and First Amendment law, the Supreme Court held that "grand juries must operate within the limits of the First Amendment as well as the Fifth."[5] Evaluating the particular case of Branzburg, the Court held that the news reporter was obligated to respond to the subpoena because he had witnessed a drug exchange and had information "directly related to criminal conduct."[6] The Supreme Court's holding is critical, however, because it recognizes the important general principle that First Amendment rights must be balanced in the determination of whether information is produced in a criminal investigation or in some other demand for production of confidential information.

In addition to First Amendment concerns, are there other grounds upon which a subpoena can be quashed?

The Supreme Court has reaffirmed that "grand juries are not licensed to engage in arbitrary fishing expeditions, nor may they select targets of investigation out of malice or an intent to harass."[7] In fact, the Court made clear that grand jury subpoenas may not be unreasonable, oppressive, indefinite, or overly burdensome.[8] Thus, when faced with a subpoena for patron information, an attorney for the library must examine the request to determine whether it is unreasonable or burdensome. Once that analysis has been made, the attorney must determine whether an argument exists that the First Amendment interests at stake outweigh any need for law enforcement to have the information.

How do Supreme Court cases dealing generally with grand jury subpoena requests apply in the context of the library?

The decision in *Branzburg* compels an analysis of the First Amendment interests. Of course, the situation presented by the facts in *Branzburg* differs starkly from the situation presented by a request for patron library use records.

Reading a book is not criminal in and of itself—unless the book itself is considered obscene, child pornography, or, in the case of minors, harmful to minors. Only a court can make the legal determination that a work is obscene, child pornography, or harmful to minors. (See chapter 3 for a definition of these terms and a complete discussion of when material is considered illegal or unprotected speech.) This analysis of privacy and confidentiality issues assumes that the book or other library material has *not* been deemed by a court to be legally obscene, child pornography, or harmful to minors. In most cases, law enforcement personnel are looking for information to corroborate a crime. However, there often is only a tenuous basis for the request and it amounts to nothing more than a fishing expedition. A person objecting to a subpoena request must file a motion with the court to "quash" the subpoena. The person thus asks the court for a ruling that he or she need not produce the requested information.

How have the courts applied *Branzburg*?

Courts have applied the *Branzburg* decision in two different ways in considering motions to quash a subpoena. Under either the majority or minority views, the first question is whether there is a First Amendment interest and a particularized harm to First Amendment principles if the information is produced. If the answer is yes, the majority of courts then ask whether the government can demonstrate that there is a compelling need for the information, whether there is some nexus between the request and the investigation, and whether there is an alternative means of obtaining the information. A minority of courts simply inquire whether there is governmental abuse such as harassment or bad faith.

How does legal counsel demonstrate that there is a First Amendment interest at stake?

As an initial matter, the library must demonstrate that there is an important right to receive information encompassed by the First Amendment. A long line of cases from the Supreme Court have held that the First Amendment protects the right to receive information.[9] That right to receive information must be balanced, therefore, with the request for information. The expectation of privacy can be demonstrated in two primary ways: (1) the library attorney should determine whether the state in which the library is located has a confidentiality provision for library patron records, which would demonstrate the recognition by the state legislature that an important privacy interest is at stake; and (2) legal counsel should secure affidavits from library personnel, library board trustees, or members of the community to show that patrons will be chilled in the exercise of their First Amendment rights if they believe that their reading habits—which are not criminal in and of themselves—can be the subject of inquiry simply in the context of a law enforcement fishing expedition.

How will the court balance the First Amendment interests against the interests of the requester?

Once a library has established that a request for patron use records has the potential to chill speech and threaten the exercise of important First Amendment rights, the court must look at the other side of the equation. Against the interests of the library and its patrons in protecting First Amendment rights, the court will balance the interests of the government (or other requester) in receiving the information from the library. At this point, the majority of federal circuit courts require the court adjudicating the matter to apply the following test: (1) whether the information sought is relevant to the investigation; (2) whether the information can be obtained by alternative means; and (3) whether there is a compelling need for the information.[10] The Fourth Circuit Court of Appeals has applied a slightly different test under *Branzburg*. The Fourth Circuit asks only whether there has been an abuse of governmental authority such as harassment or bad faith.[11] However, the court in that case stated: "We caution district courts to apply with special sensitivity, where values of expression are potentially implicated, the traditional rule that 'grand juries are not licensed to engage in arbitrary fishing expeditions, nor may they select targets of investigation out of malice or an intent to harass.'"[12] Plainly, under either application of the *Branzburg* test, First Amendment rights must be considered in the context of subpoena requests for information.

Have the courts considered specific requests to libraries?

Very few courts have been asked to consider a motion to quash by a library. Those that have considered such requests have uniformly recognized that the First Amendment interests of patrons must be considered in the context of a subpoena request for library use records. The final determination of whether a library must comply with a subpoena request has differed depending on the facts of the case.

For example, in one case a sheriff served several libraries with a request for the names of all patrons who had borrowed books on childbearing while investigating a child abandonment case. The library in that instance was located in Decatur, Texas. The library sought legal assistance and filed a motion to quash the subpoena. The court agreed with the library that the subpoena should be quashed. The court concluded that the government could not demonstrate either a compelling need or reasonable nexus between the request and the information sought. There was no basis upon which to believe that the person who had abandoned a child had borrowed a library book as an aid to giving birth to the child. The government truly was engaged in a fishing expedition. Reading a book on childbearing is not a crime. At the same time, being questioned by a law enforcement officer as to why you had borrowed a book on childbearing could cause some people embarrassment and pain.

Has a court ever ordered a library to disclose patron use information?

A court in Iowa concluded that information should be disclosed when considering a law enforcement officer's need for patron use records.[13] In that case, a law enforcement officer served the library with a subpoena seeking the names of all patrons who had borrowed any books on witchcraft. The inquiry reached the Supreme Court of Iowa. Importantly, the Supreme Court of Iowa held that a qualified privilege exists to protect library use records. In that case, an Iowa statute held that "the records of a library which, by themselves or when examined with other records, would reveal the identity of the library patron checking out or requesting an item from the library" are to be considered "confidential." The court recognized that forced disclosure of library records would chill citizens in choosing to read unpopular or controversial books. The court did not, however, quash the subpoena. The court held that the facts of the case dictated a finding that the prosecutor was entitled to the information. Regardless of whether one agrees with the court's balancing (which permitted disclosure of the information without identification of a particular suspect or requiring a more limited request for documents of a particular patron), it is important that the court recognized the need to assess the First Amendment rights of patrons in determining whether a subpoena request should be granted.

Are cases involving bookstore customer records useful to library counsel?

Yes. The issue of privacy in reading material has arisen with some frequency in the context of bookstore customer records. In 1998, in the context of his investigation of President Clinton and his alleged affair with former White House intern Monica Lewinsky, the independent counsel Kenneth Starr issued subpoenas to Kramerbooks and Barnes and Noble in Washington, D.C., seeking information about the book-buying habits of Lewinsky. The bookstores resisted, citing the same First Amendment interests applicable in the library context. The federal district court held that the First Amendment was implicated by a request for information about an individual's book purchases. The court held that the bookstores and Lewinsky demonstrated persuasively that the subpoena had a chilling effect on the exercise of First Amendment rights by bookstore customers. The bookstores demonstrated that patrons had complained about the intrusion, that sales had declined as a result of the subpoena, and that Kramerbooks had been picketed by angry patrons.

What test has been utilized by courts in evaluating whether bookstore customer use records should be disclosed?

The federal district court in the *Kramerbooks* case adopted the following test for balancing the important First Amendment interests at stake with the government's request for information: (1) whether the government could demonstrate a compelling need for the information; and (2) whether the government could demonstrate a nexus between the information sought and the grand jury investigation for which the subpoena was issued.[14] In determining that the First Amendment interests of Lewinsky had to be balanced against the independent counsel's demands for the information, the district court relied heavily on Supreme Court precedent holding that the right to receive information is a critical component of the constitutional guarantee:

> It is apparent that the materials sought by the subpoenas would disclose specific titles of books purchased by Ms. Lewinsky, whose First Amendment rights are at issue here. . . . Kramerbooks and Barnes and Noble are also engaged in constitutionally protected expressive activities. "The constitutional guarantee of freedom of the press embraces the circulation of books as well as their publication." . . . Justice Douglas emphasized the First Amendment implications of revealing an individual's book purchases: "A requirement that a publisher disclose the identity of those who buy his books, pamphlets, or papers is indeed the beginning of surveillance of the press. . . . Once the government can demand of a publisher the names of the purchasers of his publications, the free press as we know it disappears . . . the purchase of a book or pamphlet today may result in a subpoena tomorrow."[15]

The case was settled before the court was required to make the determination of whether the government had demonstrated nexus and a compelling need for the customer records. The case was settled because Lewinsky offered to make the records available on her own. The bookstores thus no longer were in the position of violating the privacy and First Amendment rights of patrons by providing customer information to a third party.

Have there been cases where the requester was not a law enforcement officer?

These issues arise in the civil context as well.[16] One such request involved Quad Graphics, a national commercial printing company with a large plant in Saratoga Springs, New York. After examining its long-distance bills, the company determined that its computers were being misused. Quad determined that employees in Saratoga Springs were able to access headquarters computers in Wisconsin and dial in to the South Adirondack Library System to access the Internet for personal purposes. Quad determined that it had incurred $23,000 in long-distance costs and lost 1,770 hours of employee time through these Internet accesses. Quad also deciphered nine 13-digit identification numbers that were used to access the library system. Quad filed a Freedom of Information Act request with the library seeking the names of the patrons holding those identification numbers. The library refused to disclose this information. Quad filed an action in court seeking to compel disclosure of the information by the library.

Have courts used a similar test in resolving cases involving requests by private parties?

In the case involving Quad Graphics, the court held that the library was not required to produce the identities of the library users. As an initial matter, the court held that New York's confidentiality statute related to library records, which protected "names or other personally identifying details" of patrons, and demonstrated the legislature's strong intent to protect this type of information from disclosure.[17] The court relied on the supporting legislative history in which the New York State Assembly stated: "The library, as the unique sanctuary of the widest possible spectrum of ideas, must protect the confidentiality of its records in order to insure its readers' right to read anything they wish, free from the fear that someone might see what they read and use this as a way to intimidate them."[18] The court held that the privilege was not absolute but that it should not grant an order of disclosure, given the clear legislative intent. The court held that to do so would be to open the door to other similar requests from parents seeking information about what their children are reading, or from spouses seeking information about what their partners are reading.

What factual research is required by legal counsel preparing a motion to quash?

Legal counsel will need to provide affidavits in support of any motion to quash a subpoena. Legal counsel should conduct the following factual investigation prior to filing a motion to quash:

- Library counsel must determine whether the library has a policy regarding the release of patron use information. Most libraries have "use policies" that address the question of library circulation and use records and explicitly protect against the release of such information.

If such a policy exists, the attorney must determine whether the policy is publicized to patrons and whether patrons rely on that policy. Legal counsel for the library should endeavor to locate patrons, library staff, and library board members who can sign affidavits attesting to the fact that patrons rely on library confidentiality policies in utilizing the library.

- Library counsel must ascertain whether library personnel, including members of the board of trustees, can attest to the fact that release of patron use information—in the absence of a compelling need—would result in a chilling effect in that patrons would be less likely to exercise their borrowing privileges.

- The library attorney should determine whether the library has adopted the Library Bill of Rights of the American Library Association. The American Library Association has a specific policy that strongly recommends that libraries—as a matter of professional standards—resist requests for confidential library patron information even if made in the form of a subpoena unless there has been a showing of good cause and a court has ordered such records disclosed.

- Library counsel should determine whether the request is overbroad and burdensome. Does the subpoena require library staff to search for documents in a warehouse? Will it take library staff days to find the documents? Does the library have sufficient staff to respond to the subpoena request? Is there an alternative method for procuring the information? Independent of the First Amendment interests at issue, the library may not have the resources to respond to a broad request for information. Even without the issue of the First Amendment, the library may move to quash the subpoena if the request is too broad or if the search for documents would be unduly burdensome.

What legal considerations must be made by an attorney preparing a motion to quash?

As library counsel begins to prepare a motion to quash, it is essential that several areas of legal research are explored:

- Counsel must ascertain whether the state in which the library is located has a confidentiality statute protecting patron records from disclosure. As is clear from the discussion of the *Quad Graphics* case above, courts will give great weight to the fact that the legislature has recognized an important privacy interest when considering whether patron use information should be disclosed. Most states offer some protection for library use records. Those statutes often appear as exemptions to the need for a government entity to provide the disclosure requested pursuant to an Open Records or Freedom of Information Act request.

- Counsel must determine whether federal or state rules governing subpoenas provide an applicable ground for quashing the subpoena that does not involve the First Amendment, such as burdensomeness or undue cost.

- A library attorney must determine how the jurisdiction in which the library is located has applied the *Branzburg v. Hayes* decision in other subpoena cases.

What should the library do if the court orders disclosure of the information?

If a court orders disclosure of patron use information, the library should consult with its legal counsel to ascertain whether an appeal is warranted. As the *Tattered Cover* case discussed earlier demonstrates, an appellate court may not agree with a lower court order to disclose information. Legal counsel will be able to analyze the likelihood of success on appeal once the lower court has issued its opinion.

NOTES

1. *Perry Ed. Assn. v. Perry Local Educators' Assn.*, 460 U.S. 37, 45 (1983).

2. *Id.*

3. *See Denver Area Educational Telecommunications Consortium, Inc. v. FCC*, 518 U.S. 727, 809 (1996) (Kennedy, J., concurring in part and dissenting in part) ("The possibility the Government could have imposed more draconian limitations on speech never has justified a lesser abridgment. Indeed, such an argument almost always is available; few of our First Amendment cases involve outright bans on speech"); *United States v. National Treasury Employees Union*, 513 U.S. 454 (1995) (invalidating a statute barring the receipt of honoraria by government employees, even though the statute did not "prohibit any speech"); *Forsyth County v. Nationalist Movement*, 505 U.S. 123 (1992) (striking down a law imposing a minimal fee on parade permits); *Simon & Schuster, Inc. v. Members of N.Y. State Crime Victims Bd.*, 502 U.S. 105 (1991) (invalidating a statute that imposed a financial burden on speech but did not ban any expression).

4. *Branzburg v. Hayes*, 408 U.S. 665 (1972).

5. *Id.* at 708.

6. *Id.*

7. *United States v. R Enterprises*, 498 U.S. 292 (1991).

8. *Id.*

9. *See Stanley v. Georgia*, 394 U.S. 557 (1969); *Lamont v. Postmaster General*, 381 U.S. 301 (1965); *NAACP v. Alabama ex rel. Patterson*, 357 U.S. 449 (1958); *Griswold v. Connecticut*, 381 U.S. 479 (1965).

10. *See, e.g., In re Grand Jury Subpoena Duces Tecum*, 78 F.3d 1307 (8th Cir.), *cert. denied*, 519 U.S. 980 (1996); *In re Grand Jury Proceedings*, 776 F.2d 1099 (2d Cir. 1985); *In re Grand Jury Proceedings*, 863 F.2d 667 (9th Cir. 1988).

11. *In re Grand Jury 87-3 Subpoena Duces Tecum*, 955 F.2d 229 (4th Cir. 1992).

12. *Id.*

13. *Brown v. Johnston*, 328 N.W. 2d 510 (Iowa), *cert. denied*, 463 U.S. 1208 (1983).

14. *In re Grand Jury Subpoena to Kramerbooks & Afterwords Inc.*, 26 Med. L. Rptr. 1599 (D.D.C. 1998).

15. *Id.* at 1600 (citing *United States v. Rumely*, 345 U.S. 41, 57 [1953] [Douglas, J., concurring]).

16. *See Quad Graphics, Inc. v. Southern Adirondack Library System*, 174 Misc. 2d 291, 664 N.Y.S. 2d 225 (N.Y. 1997).

17. *Id.*

18. *Id.*

Chapter Three

PRIVACY, CONFIDENTIALITY, AND THE INTERNET

Internet use in the library raises a number of distinct privacy issues that will be evaluated in this chapter: (1) whether Internet use records are entitled to the same privacy protections as library circulation records; (2) whether patrons are entitled to private viewing areas in the library while using the Internet; (3) whether private viewing areas or filters are necessary to protect the library from hostile work environment complaints; and (4) whether concerns about unprotected speech override the privacy interests of patrons.

Are Internet use records different for privacy purposes from library circulation records?

No. Library privacy and confidentiality policies should encompass both library circulation records for materials borrowed by patrons and Internet use records that collect information on sites accessed by patrons. The policies should cover any information that would allow someone to track the sites accessed by a particular user. Such patron data may be stored on Internet sign-up sheets, in databases on the computer, or on network databases. Thus, policies that protect patron circulation records from disclosure should be amended to include Internet use information retained in those locations. As in the context of library circulation records, the release of information related to library Internet use will inhibit patrons from using the Internet to access sensitive or controversial material. For example, a patron may need information about a medical condition but may not wish to publicize that interest. A patron will be reluctant to exercise her First Amendment rights to access information on the Internet if she believes her searches can be divulged publicly. Because patrons have a First Amendment right to access information in the library, anything that chills their access necessarily violates the Constitution because of the burden it places on the exercise of those First Amendment rights. (The discussion in chapter 2 provides guidance to the librarian and library legal counsel on steps to take if a request for Internet use information is made to the library.)

Are Internet use records protected from disclosure by statute?

Although every state provides some measure of protection for library patron records (see chapter 4), the extent to which protection is provided varies from state to state. Many states have enacted legislation that specifically designates library patron records as confidential. Because many of those statutes were drafted prior to the widespread use of the Internet, they may be phrased in such a way that Internet use records are not delineated specifically or appear to be excluded. For example, a confidentiality statute may refer to "circulation" records rather than "patron" records. Undoubtedly, at the time the legislation was drafted, the only records preserved by a library were circulation records for materials borrowed from the library. Libraries and counsel must consult their own state statutes, cases applying those statues, and attorney general opinions analyzing the statutes to determine whether there is statutory protection for Internet use records. Even if the statute does not specifically refer to Internet use records, the language may be broad enough to encompass all library patron records, whether related to books or the Internet. Legislative history that describes the goal of the legislature as the protection of privacy in broad terms can be useful. Additionally, a court case or an attorney general opinion may interpret a statute as encompassing Internet use records even in the absence of a legislative amendment specifically referring to Internet records. In sum, libraries should not conclude that the legislature intended Internet use records to be treated differently than circulation records for books simply because the Internet is not mentioned in the text of the statute.

Can Internet use records be protected in the absence of a specific privacy or confidentiality statute?

Yes. A privacy or confidentiality statute provides an additional—and important—measure of support for the argument that disclosing such information is harmful and would result in chilled speech. It is not, however, required. For example, as discussed in chapter 2, courts have extended the same privacy protection to customer records in bookstores despite the fact that no statute specifically deems bookstore customer records to be protected. The absence of a confidentiality statute or the failure of a confidentiality statute to mention Internet use records does not mean that the information must be disclosed.

Does the library owe patrons private access to the Internet?

The library is not obligated by law to provide private areas for Internet access, just as the library is not obligated by law to provide private carrels or rooms for patrons to read books. The decision to provide private areas for Internet access or private areas for research using books or periodicals is a matter of logistics, preference, and library policy. The library may make the decision to provide private areas for book or Internet research if it has the resources and space to do so and there is patron interest in having such areas. Of course, in making the policy decision of whether to provide private access to the Internet, the library should consider the differences between books and the Internet. There may be a greater need for privacy in the Internet context. A library patron may take a book home or move to a private area to read a book that the patron does not wish others to see. The Internet user does not have the same options with the Internet terminal. Nonetheless, there is no legal obligation to provide such private access.

Should the library use privacy screens, place computers in private locations, or install filters to avoid claims by library employees that they are subjected to a hostile work environment because they see images on the screen that they deem offensive?

Privacy screens and private placement of computers may help a library to avoid conflicts with patrons and employees, but whether or not to provide such private access to information on the Internet is a policy decision that each library will need to make in the context of its own resources and the needs of its employees and patrons. Some groups have advocated the additional use of filters as a way of avoiding hostile work environment complaints by employees. Pro-filter groups have argued that a hostile work environment can be created if a librarian is offended by what another employee or patron is viewing on the Internet. Other groups have advocated the use of privacy screens, recessed monitors, or private placement of computers as a means of protecting employees from images they may find offensive. To date, no court has held that the mere viewing of an image on a computer screen constitutes a hostile work environment. Neither filters nor privacy screens will insulate a library from liability, but the use of privacy screens—unlike filters—may provide a balanced approach to protecting the First Amendment rights of patrons while accommodating the needs of other patrons and employees.

What constitutes a "hostile work environment"?

Federal civil rights laws and the parallel civil rights laws of many states afford employees the right to a workplace free of discrimination. Title VII is a federal law providing that "[it] shall be an unlawful employment practice for an employer . . . to fail or refuse to hire or to discharge any individual, or otherwise to discriminate against any individual with respect to his compensation, terms, conditions, or privileges of employment because of such individual's race, color, religion, sex or national origin."[1] Many states have parallel laws. A hostile work environment exists when an employee is subjected to very specific and pervasive harassment because of the employee's race, gender, color, religion, or national origin. The inquiry into whether a hostile work environment exists is very fact-specific. In order to prove that an employer is liable for a hostile work environment, the employee initiating a lawsuit (referred to as the plaintiff) must demonstrate the following: (1) the plaintiff must be a member of a protected group (e.g., sex, race, or religion); (2) the plaintiff was subjected to *pervasive or severe harassment* because of his or her membership in a protected group; (3) the harassment unreasonably interfered with the employee's work performance; (4) both a reasonable person and the employee would view the behavior as harassment; and (5) the employer should be held responsible for the environment.[2]

Has a library ever been held liable for creating a hostile work environment due to images viewed on the Internet?

No court has specifically resolved a hostile work environment claim involving Internet images in the context of a library. Before a plaintiff may assert a hostile work environment claim in court, the complainant must file a complaint with the Equal Employment Opportunity Commission (EEOC). That agency makes an initial evaluation about the complaint and determines whether it is frivolous, worthy of consideration by a court, or so serious that it will be pursued in court by the EEOC itself on behalf of the complainant. There have been two administrative proceedings initiated by librarians alleging that a hostile work environment was created because of Internet images viewed by patrons. The two complaints were filed in administrative proceedings in Minneapolis, Minnesota, and Chicago, Illinois.

How were the Minneapolis and Chicago complaints resolved?

The Chicago complaint never progressed beyond the EEOC administrative proceedings. The Minneapolis EEOC permitted the complaint to be filed in court. This has been referred to as a finding of liability. It is not. The EEOC merely decided that the case raised a novel issue that should be considered by a court. After the complaint was filed, the parties settled the lawsuit with a monetary payment and various accommodations at the library, namely a reconfiguration of the way that patrons could print information from the Internet that would not require library staff to view the material printed.[3] Prior to the complaint proceeding, library patrons retrieved their printing requests from a central location that required the librarian to view the printed material. The hostile work environment complaint alleged that patrons were downloading and printing pornographic images purposefully so that librarians would be forced to view the printed materials when the patron retrieved them. The settlement agreement resulted in a central printing location that allowed patrons to retrieve their own materials.

Can the library be held liable for a hostile work environment if a librarian is offended by images seen on a screen as a patron or other employee is using a library computer?

Given that the harassment must be "pervasive" and "severe" in order to constitute a hostile work environment, it is questionable whether a visual image alone—viewed only in passing and not targeted in any way toward a library employee—would ever be sufficient to constitute a hostile work environment. Where cases have held that visual images have created liability, viewing of the images has been coupled with other discriminatory verbal or physical conduct. For example, one court found that a hostile work environment existed where graffiti was directed at a particular employee, sexually explicit material was placed in the employee's personal toolbox, and coworkers repeatedly made comments of a sexual nature to the employee.[4] In another case, in addition to the display of pictures, women employees were repeatedly referred to in an offensive manner, a woman employee was propositioned, materials were placed in a female employee's desk, phone calls were made to employees' homes, and cars were vandalized.[5]

When does the conduct become sufficiently pervasive to constitute a hostile work environment rather than just offensive behavior?

This is a difficult question to answer in the abstract without a specific factual scenario. Court findings related to hostile work environment claims will be very fact-specific and depend on the circumstances of the particular case. It is important to note, however, that the offensive behavior will not reach the level of a hostile work environment unless it is both pervasive *and* targeted at a particular employee. The Supreme Court has cautioned that Title VII is not a "general civility code" and that discrimination claims will not be supported by examples of "teasing." Additionally, a hostile work environment claim will not exist simply because a particular employee was offended. The behavior alleged to create a hostile work environment claim must be viewed as harassment by the employee and any reasonable person in the same situation.[6] It must be more than an isolated occurrence, must be targeted at a specific employee, and must interfere with the employee's ability to perform her job responsibilities.

Have courts evaluated the extent to which an Internet image creates a hostile work environment in contexts outside of the library?

Yes. Courts have considered various allegations of hostile work environment and have reached different results depending on the facts alleged. In one case, the court concluded that the following incidents did *not* create a hostile work environment: (1) one incident in which the plaintiff opened an envelope for her supervisor marked "personal and confidential" and found pornographic pictures; and (2) during screening of her supervisor's e-mail, the plaintiff identified a total of twelve e-mails over a period of seventeen months that included sixteen text-only sexual jokes and one cartoon with dragons "apparently" mating. The court concluded that because her work responsibilities "did not require her to handle jokes and other non-work-related materials, she could easily have elected not to read these e-mails after she had ascertained that they were jokes." The court noted particularly that the e-mails and mailing could not constitute "severe and pervasive harassment" where there was no contention or evidence that the mail was "targeted" at her but rather appeared clearly to be directed at her supervisor.[7]

In another case, a professor claimed that he was subjected to a hostile work environment when he logged onto his computer and found two icons that, once opened, were "offensive." He viewed each for a few seconds. The court held that "pictures of a sexual nature do not rise to the level of sexual harassment." The district court also held that the incident did not constitute "severe and pervasive" harassment where it was "uncontradicted" that the professor "viewed the pictures for only a matter of seconds and that the pictures remained on his computer for a matter of days."[8]

Can the library be held liable for the acts of a supervisor?

Yes. The library can be held liable for the acts of a supervisor if the employer failed to exercise reasonable care to prevent or correct the harassment. Two Supreme Court cases—*City of Boca Raton* and *Burlington Industries*—reaffirm that an employer can be vicariously liable without ever knowing of the harassment. The Court held, however, that the employer can raise two affirmative defenses: (1) that the employer exercised reasonable care to prevent and promptly correct any sexually harassing behavior; and (2) that the plaintiff unreasonably failed to take advantage of any preventive or corrective opportunities provided by the employer or otherwise failed to avoid harm.[9] Every library should, therefore, have a sexual harassment policy that provides a private grievance and investigation system for complaints by employees.

Can the library be held responsible for the acts of a patron or another non-supervisory employee?

Yes. The library can be held responsible for the acts of a patron or another non-supervisory employee if the employer acted in a negligent manner. Courts have held employers liable for the harassment of customers or other employees if a manager knew, or in the exercise of reasonable care should have known, that the harassment existed in the workplace.[10] In other words, once a manager or supervisor becomes aware of a potential situation of harassment by another employee or patron, the manager must take action to investigate the complaint and eliminate the harassment to prevent employer liability.

In the context of a hostile work environment claim, do courts consider the First Amendment implications of the claim?

Yes. The First Amendment rights of other employees or patrons will be a factor that a court will balance against the allegations that certain conduct or words create a hostile work environment. For example, in evaluating a policy banning the possession of *Playboy* magazine in a fire department to protect against hostile work environment claims, the court applied a balancing test and concluded that the policy violated the First Amendment rights of the firefighters. The court concluded that the First Amendment rights of the firefighters were violated to the extent that the policy prohibited the private possession, reading, and consensual sharing of the magazine at the workplace despite the fact that its presence at the workplace might offend other employees.[11] By contrast, another court found that the presence of pornographic magazines could be considered as contributing to a hostile work environment where it was coupled with the display of nude pictures and movies throughout the firehouse with no ability for an employee to avoid them.[12] In sum, courts will balance the First Amendment rights of patrons and employees in the factual analysis of whether a hostile work environment claim has been created.

Does a library employee offended by certain reading material have the right to refuse to handle that material in the context of her job responsibilities?

Although this issue has not arisen in the context of a case involving libraries, analogous situations offer strong guidance to libraries that might be confronted with an employee refusing to shelve or catalog library materials she finds offensive or otherwise declining to complete an employment task.

For example, one court considered the claim of a plaintiff discharged from her job at a grocery store for refusing to stock and sell adult magazines. She contended that the action of selling the magazines would violate her "Christian principles" and argued that the job requirement created a hostile work environment if the store owner did not put opaque covers on the magazines. Although she also alleged that male customers made "lewd" and sexually suggestive comments to her about the magazines on three occasions, the district court rejected her claim. The court concluded that the store had a First Amendment right to sell the magazines and the employee did not have the right to dictate whether or how legally protected materials would be sold to the public.[13] A different result might have been reached by the court if a customer, with the knowledge of the store owner, repeatedly used the materials to target the plaintiff with lewd suggestions in a pervasive manner that prevented her from fulfilling her job responsibilities. In the absence of such pervasive and targeted harassment, however, the store owner did not have an obligation to accommodate the store clerk's religious beliefs. Similar principles would apply in the context of a library if an employee refused to carry out his job responsibilities on the ground that materials in the library offended his principles.

Ultimately, do filters provide the library with a way to protect the privacy interests of its employees and a means to avoid employee lawsuits?

Filters are not a means to avoid lawsuits for several reasons. First, filters cannot guarantee that offensive material will be blocked. Second, filters cannot stop sexual or racial harassment if an employee or patron is intent upon such behavior. If someone is determined to harass a library staff employee, they can do so without using Internet images. If an employee wants to harass another employee or a patron wants to harass an employee, they can do so with books, materials brought from home, verbal assaults, or physical conduct. Filters cannot protect employees from hostile work environment situations. Additionally, broadly applied filters will result in constitutionally protected material being blocked. This poses a serious First Amendment concern without any assurance whatsoever that the filter will protect the library from hostile work environment suits.

Do filters offer immunity from liability for a hostile work environment claim?

While the library may choose privacy screens or private placement of computers as a means of avoiding employee discontent over Internet use by patrons or other staff, the decision to filter raises serious constitutional issues that could subject the library to liability for violating the First Amendment rights of patrons. Although the library is not under a legal obligation to use privacy screens or place computers in private areas of the library, both options certainly are preferable and less restrictive alternatives to eliminating access to the Internet or to installing filters.

Are there steps a library can take to minimize its potential liability for hostile work environment suits?

There are several steps that a library can—and should—take to fulfill its responsibility as an employer and to prevent a finding of liability for any alleged hostile work environment.

First, every library should adopt a harassment policy, with the advice of counsel, that makes clear that the library does not condone, encourage, or tolerate the harassment of employees by other employees or by patrons through the use of any means, whether or not those means include images from the Internet.

Second, the library should publicize its sexual harassment or hostile work environment policy by posting it prominently in the library so that every employee and patron is aware of its existence.

Third, libraries should establish confidential procedures for addressing complaints of a hostile work environment by an employee.

Fourth, libraries must make those procedures easily accessible and well known to employees. The library must ensure that every current employee receives a copy of that policy and all new employees receive the policy when they begin their employment.

Fifth, if a complaint comes in, it should immediately be directed to the employment counselor or legal counsel for investigation, regardless of whether or not it appears to be meritorious. The investigation and complaint procedure can be conducted privately and confidentially. The person or committee designated to conduct the investigation must determine if the complaint has merit.

Sixth, as an optional step the library may consider whether it should locate Internet terminals in private areas of the library or use privacy screens. This is not required by law. This is a policy decision a library can make to minimize complaints by employees.

Can a claim of hostile work environment be brought by a library patron?

No. A sexual harassment or hostile work environment claim can only be made by an employee.

Can the library be sued by a patron offended by images seen on the Internet?

Although there is never a guarantee that a lawsuit can be avoided—even if frivolous—to date no court has found a library liable for permitting unfiltered access to pornographic images. In a case originating in California, a woman sued a public library claiming that her twelve-year-old son was able to view and download pornography at the public library. The plaintiff's claims were summarily rejected, based in part on a provision in the federal Communications Decency Act that immunizes service providers against state law liability for third parties' postings.[14]

The court also rejected the plaintiff's allegation that the library exhibits obscenity or material harmful to minors by allowing computer use: "Any such implication would be contrary to the library policy attached to the complaint, which among other things, prohibits the use of computer resources for illegal purposes." The court also rejected the plaintiff's conclusory allegation that the librarians help minors to access obscenity and material harmful to minors because "such lessons would not further the library's stated mission, and would not be consistent with its policy that computers are to be used only for 'educational, informational and recreational purposes.'"[15]

Is pornography protected by the First Amendment?

All speech is protected by the First Amendment with the exception of three types of unprotected or illegal speech: (1) obscenity, (2) material harmful to minors, and (3) child pornography.

Is "sexually explicit" or "violent" speech considered unprotected speech?

No. Various states have attempted to criminalize the distribution of violent or sexually explicit speech in the context of statutes banning access to video games by minors. Courts uniformly have held that violent or sexually explicit speech that does not cross the line to obscenity, material harmful to minors, or child pornography is protected by the First Amendment.[16]

What is "obscenity"?

Federal, state, or local laws may prohibit the distribution of obscenity. Whether a particular work constitutes obscenity is a fact-based inquiry. For many years, the Supreme Court utilized a "we know it when we see it" approach to determining whether material crossed the line from protected speech to obscene speech.[17] In 1973 the Supreme Court established a three-part test to be utilized by judges or juries in determining whether material is obscene.

The fact-finder (which is the jury unless the defendant in a particular case has waived his right to have the case heard by the jury and allows the judge to make the determination) must determine: (1) whether the average person, applying "contemporary community standards," would find that the work, as a whole, appeals to the "prurient interest"; (2) whether the work depicts or describes, in a patently offensive way, sexual conduct specifically defined by the applicable state law; and (3) whether the work, taken as a whole, lacks serious literary, artistic, political, or scientific value.[18] The "prurient interest" and "patent offensiveness" questions require the fact-finder to determine whether the work is obscene in a particular community. Thus, a jury in one part of the country could find that a work was obscene while a jury in another location could conclude that the work was protected by the First Amendment. The "serious value" test requires application of a national standard. If the work has "serious value," then it cannot be deemed obscene in any part of the country.

What material is deemed "harmful to minors"?

Federal or state law may also criminalize the distribution of material that is "harmful to minors" or "harmful to juveniles." The statutory definitions will vary from jurisdiction to jurisdiction. Essentially, however, the determination of whether material constitutionally can be deemed "harmful to minors" parallels the obscenity test. The fact-finder tasked with determining whether the material is constitutionally "harmful to minors" must consider whether the material is "patently offensive" for minors, whether it appeals to a minor's prurient interest, and whether it has serious value for minors.[19]

Will material be deemed "harmful" for all minors if it is found to be "harmful" for younger minors?

No. Courts have held that a determination of whether material is "harmful to minors" must be made in the context of whether the material would be harmful to the oldest of minors. In other words, material cannot be deemed harmful to minors if it would be constitutionally protected for a seventeen-year-old even if one might conclude that it was "harmful" for a five-year-old. If the material would not be considered "patently offensive" to a teenager or has "serious value" for teenagers, then it cannot constitutionally be deemed unprotected speech.[20]

What is "child pornography"?

Federal, state, or local jurisdictions may also prohibit the distribution of child pornography. Child pornography is defined as the portrayal of actual children engaged in actual sexual activity.[21] The obscenity test does not apply to this type of unprotected speech and there is no inquiry into whether the material has "serious value." If the material constitutes child pornography, then it cannot have serious value.

Is "virtual child pornography" unprotected speech?

No. The Supreme Court has concluded that "virtual" child pornography, whether generated by computer or by using young-looking adults as actors, does not constitute unprotected speech. Principles of free speech require that child pornography is defined as actual children engaged in actual sexual activity.[22]

Do public library patrons have a privacy or First Amendment interest in accessing illegal speech on Internet terminals?

No. Because work that is deemed obscene, harmful to minors, or child pornography constitutes unprotected or illegal speech, there is no First Amendment right in having access to those types of speech in the library. Illegal speech is not constitutionally protected. But how can library staff ascertain whether material is illegal? In short, they cannot. Patrons do have a right to access sexually explicit speech that does not reach the level of obscenity. Only a jury or judge in an actual criminal case can make the determination of whether material meets the three-part obscenity test. Thus, library staff cannot make this determination without the benefit of an adversarial hearing and legal instructions from the court. In sum, therefore, while patrons do not have the right to access illegal speech in the library, it will be impossible for library staff to determine whether a particular work is illegal or not.

Is child pornography easier to recognize than obscenity?

It may be. Definitions will vary from jurisdiction to jurisdiction. The definitions of child pornography, however, tend to be clearer than those encompassing obscenity. Since child pornography is defined as actual children engaged in actual sexual activity and is not subject to a community standards analysis, library staff may be able to easily identify this type of illegal material. Moreover, some statutes may impose an obligation to report child pornography. The library should consult with counsel to determine whether there is an obligation to report observed instances of child pornography. If so, then the library should consult with the local prosecutor's office for guidance on how to train staff to fulfill their obligations without imposing on the privacy rights of patrons engaged in exercising their constitutionally protected rights under the First Amendment.

Does the library have an obligation under federal law to restrict access to images that are obscene, harmful to minors, or child pornography?

The federal Children's Internet Protection Act (CIPA) requires that libraries accepting certain types of e-rate funds and grants install filters that will restrict access to visual images that are obscene, harmful to minors, or child pornography.[23] The statute provides that a library administrator may disable the software to enable access for "*bona fide* research or other lawful purposes." This statute was challenged, and the Supreme Court held it was constitutional based on the government's representation that libraries would disable such filters for all adults without the need for the patron to demonstrate a bona fide or other lawful interest in the material.[24] The statute does not require a guarantee that no patron will access unprotected speech on a library's Internet terminals. Nor could it. Filters overblock and underblock. In other words, because a filter is not a judge or jury applying contemporary community standards as required by the Supreme Court for determinations of whether material is obscene or harmful to minors, it provides only a guess as to whether the material is unprotected speech. Filters are not designed to apply legal standards. Filters are designed to apply to broad categories of speech. Filters will block legal speech that is constitutionally protected. Nor can filters capture all speech that is unprotected. Thus, the CIPA statute does not require a guarantee that all unprotected speech will be blocked—merely a certification that a filter is in place. Filters are only required if the library accepts the particular funds covered by the statute.

Does the library have an obligation under state or local law to restrict access to images that are obscene, harmful to minors, or child pornography?

Libraries, with the assistance of counsel, should monitor their state statutes and local ordinances to determine whether their state or local jurisdictions have imposed any CIPA-type requirements that would impose a burden on the library to filter Internet access. Various state legislatures have considered such legislative funding requirements.

If a library is not obligated by CIPA or a similar local law to place filters on its computers, should libraries attempt to prevent access to obscenity, material harmful to minors, or child pornography since such speech is illegal?

It would be impossible for library staff to determine with any degree of accuracy that a particular work is illegal on the grounds that it is obscene or harmful to minors. Material is not deemed obscene or harmful to minors until a jury (or judge acting as fact-finder) makes the determination that the material lacks serious value and, based on contemporary community standards, appeals to the prurient interest in a patently offensive manner. Library staff cannot make this legal determination. Library staff cannot act as the arbiters of contemporary community standards without the benefit of an adversary hearing and adequate instruction from a judge as to the applicable law. As a consequence, library staff restricting access to material on the ground that it is illegal may instead block access to constitutionally protected material. Restricting access to constitutionally protected material may subject the library to a lawsuit alleging a violation of First Amendment rights.

Is there any point to having a policy that prohibits access to illegal speech if librarians cannot identify which speech is illegal?

Yes. Every library should include in its Internet use policy a statement that the library does not permit use of library equipment to access material that is obscene, harmful to minors, or child pornography. Although library staff may not be able to ascertain if a particular work is illegal, patrons have an obligation not to use library equipment for illegal purposes, and the library should make clear that it prohibits such use. In at least one case, such a policy helped a library to avoid liability when a minor accessed pornography at the library and his mother sued the library for harming her child. The court rejected the mother's allegation that the library exhibits obscenity or material harmful to minors by allowing computer use: "Any such implication would be contrary to the library policy attached to the complaint, which among other things, prohibits the use of computer resources for illegal purposes."[25]

Does the library have an obligation to report obscenity, material harmful to minors, or child pornography to law enforcement authorities?

Libraries should consult with their counsel to determine whether a reporting obligation exists under their local law.

How should library staff respond if one patron complains about Internet images accessed by another patron?

Some libraries utilize a "tap on the shoulder" policy to respond to patron complaints that another patron is viewing material that is "offensive." When one patron complains about the Internet images being viewed by another patron, library staff will ask the person to stop viewing the site. This practice is risky. As discussed previously, librarians are not equipped to ascertain whether a particular work is illegal. If librarians ask a patron to exit a site that contains constitutionally protected material, then the library may be at risk of a lawsuit alleging violation of the patron's constitutional rights. Libraries with frequent complaints from patrons about other patrons' viewing habits should consider rearranging the placement of terminals or using recessed computers or privacy screens as a means of allowing patrons access to constitutionally protected material without offense to others. If those options are not feasible, then the library should consider resolving patron complaints by asking the complaining party to move to another terminal rather than asking a patron to refrain from accessing a particular site.

NOTES

1. 42 U.S.C. § 2000e-2(a) (2000).
2. *Meritor Savings Bank v. Vinson*, 477 U.S. 57 (1986).
3. There are no court decisions in the Chicago or Minneapolis cases because the complaint was never filed in court in Chicago and the matter was settled prior to trial in the Minneapolis case.
4. *Robinson v. Jacksonville Shipyards, Inc.*, 760 F. Supp. 1486 (M.D. Florida).
5. *Andrews v. City of Philadelphia*, 895 F.2d 1469 (3d Cir. 1990).
6. *Faragher v. City of Boca Raton*, 524 U.S. 775 (1998).
7. *Hoffman v. Lincoln Life and Annuity Distributors, Inc.*, 174 F. Supp. 2d 367 (D. Md. 2001).
8. *Lutz v. Purdue University*, 133 F. Supp. 2d 1101 (N.D. Ill. 2001).
9. *Faragher v. City of Boca Raton*, 524 U.S. 775 (1998); *Burlington Industries, Inc. v. Ellerth*, 524 U.S. 742 (1998).
10. See, e.g., *Lockard v. Pizza Hut, Inc.*, 162 F.3d 1062 (10th Cir. 1998) (holding that an employer can be held liable for sexual harassment caused by customers if the employer failed to remedy a hostile working environment that managers knew, or in the exercise of reasonable care should have known, existed in the workplace); *Quinn v. Green Tree Credit Corp.*, 159 F.3d 759 (2d Cir. 1998) (holding that a plaintiff alleging harassment by co-employees or customers must show either that the employer provided no reasonable avenue of complaint or knew of the harassment but failed to address it); *Folkerson v. Circus Circus Enterprises, Inc.*, 107 F.3d 754 (9th Cir. 1997) (holding that the employer of a casino employee could be held liable for the actions of a casino patron "where the employer ratifies or acquiesces in the harassment by not taking immediate and/or corrective actions when it knew or should have known of the conduct)"; *Powell v. Las Vegas Hilton Corp.*, 841 F. Supp. 1024 (D. Nev. 1992) (holding that an employer could be held liable for the sexual harassment of employees by nonemployees, including customers).
11. *Johnson v. County of Los Angeles Fire Dept.*, 865 F. Supp. 1430 (C.D. Cal. 1994).
12. *O'Rourke v. City of Providence*, 235 F.3d 713 (1st Cir. 2001).
13. *Stanley v. The Lawson Co.*, 993 F. Supp 1084 (N.D. Ohio 1997).

14. 47 U.S.C. § 230 (1998).

15. *Kathleen R. v. City of Livermore*, 87 Cal. App. 4th 684, 104 Cal. Rptr. 2d 772 (Cal. Ct. App. 2001).

16. *Interactive Digital Software Assn. v. St. Louis County*, 329 F.3d 954 (8th Cir. 2003); *James v. Meow Media, Inc.*, 300 F.3d 683 (6th Cir. 2002), *cert. denied*, 537 U.S. 1159 (2003); *American Amusement Mach. Assn. v. Kendrick*, 244 F.3d 572 (7th Cir. 2001), *cert. denied*, 534 U.S. 994 (2001); *ESA v. Blagojevich*, 404 F. Supp. 2d 1051 (N.D. Ill. 2005); *VSDA v. Schwarzenegger*, 401 F. Supp. 2d 1034 (N.D. Cal. 2005); *ESA v. Granholm*, 404 F. Supp. 2d 978 (E.D. Mich. Nov. 9, 2005); *Video Software Dealers Assn. v. Maleng*, 325 F. Supp. 2d 1180 (W.D. Wash. 2004).

17. *Jacobellis v. Ohio*, 378 U.S. 184 (1964) (Stewart, J., concurring).

18. *Miller v. California*, 413 U.S. 15 (1973).

19. *Ginsberg v. New York*, 390 U.S. 629 (1968).

20. *American Booksellers Assn. v. Virginia*, 882 F.2d 125, 127 (4th Cir. 1989), *cert. denied*, 494 U.S. 1056 (1990); and *American Booksellers v. Webb*, 919 F.2d 1493, 1504–5 (11th Cir. 1990), *cert. denied*, 500 U.S. 942 (1991).

21. *New York v. Ferber*, 458 U.S. 747 (1982).

22. *Ashcroft v. Free Speech Coalition*, 535 U.S. 234 (2002).

23. Children's Internet Protection Act, codified at 47 U.S.C. § 254(h) (2002).

24. *United States v. American Library Association*, 539 U.S. 194 (2003).

25. *Kathleen R. v. City of Livermore*, 87 Cal. App. 4th 684, 104 Cal. Rptr. 2d 772 (Cal. Ct. App. 2001).

Chapter Four

STATE PRIVACY AND CONFIDENTIALITY STATUTES

Pursuant to Open Records laws and Freedom of Information laws, government institutions are required to respond to public requests for information about the workings of the institution. Those same laws, however, provide exemptions for certain categories of documents. Virtually every state provides some protection for library records.

The appendix in this book contains a survey and summary of pertinent provisions related to the confidentiality of library patron records. The following discussion of state privacy laws is based on a review of the statutes included in that appendix. **The survey and discussion of particular statutes must be updated by researchers as issues arise. State laws may be amended at any time**. Librarians and lawyers responding to a request for information or evaluating the library policies applicable to patron records must research current state statutes to determine whether the law included in the appendix or discussed in this chapter is still in effect.

Inclusion of the appendix in this book and a discussion of state laws serve two purposes. First, the appendix's survey summarizing state confidentiality laws is designed to guide the librarian or lawyer quickly to the right place to look for the current law in their state when confronted by a request for library patron records. The restatement of the law in the appendix should serve merely as a guide for further legal research. Laws are amended constantly. **The researcher must determine if the legal language appearing here is still in effect at the time of the particular request for records**. The appendix is designed merely to serve as a starting point for further research.

Second, the state survey may be useful to librarians and legal counsel in evaluating the law in their own state as compared to the laws in other states. Thus, the survey could serve as a guide to further state legislative efforts by providing librarians and lawyers with an efficient method of evaluating whether the law in their particular state is broad enough to provide adequate protection to library patron records.

Does every state provide protection for library circulation records through a state statute?

With the exception of Hawaii and Kentucky, every state provides some protection for library circulation records through a state statute. In Hawaii and Kentucky, Attorney General Opinion Letters provide direction to libraries and take the position that library patrons have a privacy interest in their library circulation records. Whether through statute or attorney general opinion, the extent to which protection is provided for such records varies in each state.

Even if a state provides that records are confidential, is the library required to provide parents with the records of their minor children?

Most state statutes do not differentiate between adults and minors. If a state statute generally provides protection for library circulation records, then that protection should apply to minors as well. If a state has a general privacy protection for patron records, the library should not divulge patron information to anyone other than the patron. Several states, including Alabama, Alaska, Louisiana, South Dakota, Utah, West Virginia, Wisconsin, and Wyoming, currently provide libraries with an explicit directive to allow parents access to minors' records. In Colorado, parents can access their child's records if they have the minor's account number. In New Mexico, the state legislature has provided that parents can access the school library records of their children but has not extended that access to public library records. Florida permits a library to disclose a minor's circulation record to a parent in order to collect a fine.

What if the parent needs to see the record to pay an outstanding fine for overdue books?

In a state that does not give parents explicit access to their minors' records, the library should not disclose that information to anyone other than the minor patron. Libraries should use their regular method of pursuing compensation for overdue materials, such as sending an overdue notice to the home of the patron. The parent will need to coordinate with the minor to pay the outstanding fine.

Are parents given more access to school library records?

Only one state—New Mexico—explicitly differentiates between school libraries and public libraries by allowing parents access to school library records.

If the confidentiality statute in my state provides that the library may disclose patron record information in response to a subpoena, is my library obligated to disclose that material?

No. Some statutes provide that the library "may" disclose information in response to a subpoena, but they do not compel the library to disclose such information. If the library has a confidentiality policy related to patron records, then it should contact an attorney to review the subpoena and determine whether the records should be produced. A subpoena is not a court order. It is simply a request from a law enforcement official or attorney in a private matter seeking such information in relation to a court case or investigation. The subpoena may be overbroad and violate the confidentiality provision of the library.

What is the difference between a subpoena and a search warrant?

A search warrant is a court order directing law enforcement personnel to search a particular place for particular information. The person or entity to which a search warrant is directed cannot refuse to comply with the warrant. A subpoena is merely a request for records, not a court order to produce records.

If a law enforcement officer comes to my library with a search warrant, must I let him search information about patron records?

Yes. You can ask the officer to wait until you have called an attorney, but the officer does not have to comply with that request. You should nonetheless call your attorney and ask her to arrive as soon as possible. An attorney can review the warrant for legality and can ensure that it is executed as required by the court. If the law enforcement officer will not wait for an attorney, then review the warrant carefully and observe the search to ensure that the officer searches only the records permitted by the court. If, for example, the warrant only allows the search of one computer, be sure that only one computer is searched.

If a law enforcement officer comes to my library with a subpoena, must I disclose the requested information?

No. A subpoena is not a court order and has not been reviewed by a judge. A subpoena is merely a request for records. The law enforcement officer should be informed that the library attorney will be notified of the request and will respond to the officer's request. The library should, however, at this point ensure that the requested information is retained even if it would have been destroyed in the ordinary course of business.

Is there any situation in which a law enforcement officer could seize information without a search warrant or subpoena?

Yes. There are two instances in which law enforcement officers could seize information without a warrant and without making a subpoena request. First, an officer may seize evidence without a warrant in "exigent circumstances," where the officer believes that failing to seize the evidence will result in physical harm to someone or destruction of the evidence and it is impossible to obtain a warrant before such harm results. If such a seizure is challenged in court, the judge will consider whether a reasonable person would have acted in the same manner. Second, an officer may seize evidence that is in "plain view." If, for example, an officer saw a crime being committed and saw evidence of the crime without a search, then the evidence could be seized.

Should a library disclose records to law enforcement if the crime has been committed at the library?

In all instances in which a request for patron records has been made, the library attorney must be consulted. If a patron has engaged in theft or vandalism, witnesses can assist law enforcement in apprehending the right individual without the need to disclose circulation records or other records whose disclosure would impact First Amendment rights. Only the state of Louisiana provides an exemption to the confidentiality provisions for actual crimes witnessed by a librarian or patron and reported in a specified manner to law enforcement.

Are surveillance cameras at the library subject to the restrictions imposed by confidentiality statutes?

A library may need to use surveillance cameras to prevent theft, vandalism, or crimes against other patrons on the premises. The library must, however, ensure that the placement of the cameras does not reveal the reading or library material choices of patrons. For example, surveillance cameras should not be placed behind the circulation desk if they would reveal the books that patrons are borrowing or behind computers in a manner that would reveal the sites visited by a patron.

If library circulation information is disclosed in violation of a state confidentiality statute, will the librarian face any consequences?

In some states, disclosure of confidential information can lead to criminal fines or civil penalties. Criminal fines can be imposed in Arizona, Colorado, the District of Columbia, Montana, Rhode Island, and South Carolina. Some states, such as Michigan, Montana, New Mexico, and Rhode Island, permit the person whose record was disclosed to file a civil suit for penalties.

If the library receives a request for patron information, should the patron be informed of the request?

In most cases, the person to whom a request for records was directed will also be asked to refrain from revealing the request to prevent criminal obstruction by the target of the investigation. These types of requests commonly are referred to as "gag orders." An attorney should be consulted prior to any publication of the request. Only the District of Columbia explicitly requires that patrons be informed if their records are requested. The District of Columbia statute has a specific notice procedure that must be followed if a request for patron information is received by the library.

Should libraries have record destruction policies?

Yes. Libraries should have a record destruction policy in place to purge records that are not needed. Personally identifiable information about patrons should be destroyed as soon as the library no longer needs that information for the efficient operation of the library. For example, many libraries have a system in place that retains information pertaining to the materials borrowed by a patron only until those materials are returned. The library has no need to know that a particular patron borrowed a particular book once the book has been returned. The library system could, however, retain the information that a particular book was borrowed ten times in the last year without retaining the names of the person who borrowed the materials. Statistical information about the number of times a book was borrowed that does not reveal personally identifiable information about patrons can be useful to the efficient operation of the library and resource allocation decisions.

Chapter Five

MINORS' FIRST AMENDMENT RIGHTS AND RIGHTS TO PRIVACY

This chapter examines minors' rights to privacy through an analysis of general First Amendment principles. The courts have recognized that minors have First Amendment rights, although those rights are not coextensive with the rights of adults. The rights of minors may also differ depending on the context—the public library as opposed to the school library.

Do minors have First Amendment rights?

The U.S. Supreme Court has long recognized that minors enjoy some degree of First Amendment protection. It was well established in the landmark *Tinker* case that students do not "shed their constitutional rights to freedom of speech or expression at the schoolhouse gate."[1] In *Tinker*, the Supreme Court concluded that a public school ban on students wearing black armbands in protest of the Vietnam War was unconstitutional. The Court explained its holding by noting that "in our system, students may not be regarded as closed-circuit recipients of only that which the State chooses to communicate."[2] More recently, an appellate court considering the constitutionality of an ordinance restricting minors' access to certain video arcade games echoed the *Tinker* court's admonition that minors must have a broad range of information for intellectual growth, holding that "people are unlikely to become well-functioning, independent-minded adults and responsible citizens if they are raised in an intellectual bubble."[3] Building on the recognition that access to information is fundamentally necessary for the intellectual maturity of children, courts have held that minors' First Amendment liberties include the right to receive information and plainly extend beyond schools.

Do minors have the same First Amendment rights as adults?

No. The Supreme Court has limited minors' right to receive information in two instances in which adults' constitutional rights remain broader: (1) public schools have the latitude to restrict access to books deemed "educationally unsuitable" for students; and (2) states may deem certain materials "obscene" for minors (even if the materials are protected for adults) and criminalize the distribution of such materials to minors.

How much discretion do school officials have to determine that materials are "educationally unsuitable"?

Courts have given public schools significant latitude to restrict minors' receipt of information if the school's judgment is based *objectively* on the fact that information is "educationally unsuitable" rather than on an official's *subjective* disagreement with or disapproval of the content of the information. In the landmark case of *Board of Education v. Pico*, the Supreme Court considered whether a public school had impermissibly removed a number of books from the school library. A majority of the Court held that the removal was unconstitutional. The test utilized by the *Pico* plurality opinion has been applied repeatedly by courts wrestling with the question of whether book censorship is unconstitutional: book removals are unconstitutional if the decision to restrict access is based on the ideas the books expressed and are permissible if officials were motivated by concerns that the books were "educationally unsuitable" or "pervasively vulgar."[4] The plurality also recognized that schools must have substantial discretion in designing curricula.[5]

CASE STUDY: *BOARD OF EDUCATION V. PICO*

The Supreme Court considered whether a local school board violated the Constitution by removing books from a school library, such as *Slaughterhouse Five* and *Soul on Ice* (*Board of Education v. Pico*, 457 U.S. 853 [1982]). The Court reiterated the well-established principle that local school boards have broad discretion to manage school affairs, particularly decisions regarding curriculum issues. The Court also held, however, that "the right to receive ideas is a necessary predicate to the *recipient's* meaningful exercise of his own rights of speech, press, and political freedom" (*id.* at 867). The Court held, moreover, that the school board's absolute discretion over matters of curriculum is "misplaced where, as here, they attempt to extend their claim of absolute discretion beyond the compulsory environment of the classroom, into the school library and the regime of voluntary inquiry that there holds sway" (*id.* at 869). The Court held finally that "if petitioners *intended* by their removal decision to deny respondents access to ideas with which petitioners disagreed, and if this intent was the decisive factor in petitioner's decision, then petitioners have exercised their discretion in violation of the Constitution" (*id.* at 871, emphasis added).

Is the removal of material from the children's room of a public library to the adult section of the library censorship?

A court in Texas considered this question and held that the removal of books from the children's room to the adult section of the library was an impermissible burden on the First Amendment rights of the children and their parents.[6] The city council of Wichita Falls had passed a resolution that allowed books to be removed from the children's section of the public library through a petition signed by 300 library cardholders. This mechanism was used to remove *Daddy's Roommate* and *Heather Has Two Mommies.* The court held that the library is a limited public forum and that the books could not be constitutionally removed from the children's room based on the petitioners' disagreement with the content and views expressed in those books. The court held that the First Amendment was violated despite the fact that the books were not removed from the library entirely because "the burdens on Plaintiffs' First Amendment rights imposed by the Resolution are nonetheless constitutionally objectionable."[7] The court held that the removal placed significant burdens on the ability of children and their parents to find the books while browsing in the children's section of the library.

Can the library require parental permission before a minor can borrow certain books?

A court in Arkansas rejected a school's requirement that minors have parental permission prior to reading or borrowing Harry Potter books.[8] The Cedarville School District had removed Harry Potter books from general circulation and only permitted student access with parental permission. The district court held that the removal from general circulation was unconstitutional because it impermissibly burdened the minors' access to constitutionally protected material. School officials could not prove that the books were "educationally unsuitable," and thus minors had the right to access those materials without any restrictions on access.

What restrictions are permissible on the ground that material is "harmful to minors"?

Government entities also may restrict minors' right to receive information that the state has deemed "obscene" for minors even if the materials are protected for adults. In the *Ginsberg* case, the Supreme Court upheld the conviction of a magazine vendor for selling an adult magazine to a sixteen-year-old. The Court explained that although the magazine clearly was not "obscene" for adults, the state constitutionally was permitted to adopt a distinct, broader definition of "obscenity" for minors.[9] Because obscene speech enjoys no First Amendment protection, under *Ginsberg* states may completely bar minors from receiving material deemed obscene for them but not for adults. Accordingly, most states have enacted "harmful to minors" obscenity statutes. (See chapter 3 for definitions and an explanation of "harmful to minors" statutes.)

Does the library have an obligation to restrict minors' access to material that is deemed "harmful to minors"?

As explained in more detail in chapter 3, the determination of whether material is harmful to minors is subject to a three-part test: (1) whether the average person, applying "contemporary community standards," would find that the work, as a whole, appeals to the "prurient interest" of minors; (2) whether the work depicts or describes, in a patently offensive way for minors, sexual conduct specifically defined by the applicable state law; and (3) whether the work, taken as a whole, lacks serious literary, artistic, political, or scientific value. Material may only be deemed "harmful to minors" by a jury or judge evaluating the material as a whole and pursuant to contemporary community standards. Material could be deemed "harmful" to minors in one community and acceptable in another. Library staff thus cannot make an assessment of whether material meets the legal definition of "harmful to minors." If the jurisdiction in which a library is located has a "harmful to minors" statute, the library should have a policy that prohibits patrons from accessing all illegal speech on the Internet terminals in the library, including material that is "harmful to minors."

Do minors have the right to access "indecent" speech?

In *FCC v. Pacifica Foundation*, the Supreme Court permitted restrictions on the broadcast of speech that was merely "indecent," not "obscene as to minors" under *Ginsberg*.[10] The Court's reasoning focused largely on the claim that children might hear the indecent speech in a broadcast medium.[11] The Court, however, has declined to extend *Pacifica* to other media, including telephone communications and, most notably, the Internet.[12]

Are minors prohibited from access to nudity?

Courts have recognized limits on the *Ginsberg* principle that certain material is "harmful" for minors even if it is not obscene for adults. For example, the Supreme Court has made clear that states may not simply ban minors' exposure to a full category of speech, such as nudity, when only a subset of that category can plausibly be deemed "obscene" for them.[13] For example, a jury could not plausibly conclude that a medical book or art book with nudity constitutes material harmful to minors because such books have "serious value" for minors.

Will material be deemed "harmful" for all minors if it is found to be "harmful" for younger minors?

No. Courts have held that a determination of whether material is "harmful to minors" must be made in the context of whether the material would be harmful to the oldest of minors. In other words, material cannot be deemed harmful to minors if it would be constitutionally protected for a seventeen-year-old even if one might conclude that it was "harmful" for a five-year-old. If the material would not be considered "patently offensive" to a teenager or has "serious value" for teenagers, then it cannot constitutionally be deemed unprotected speech.[14]

Do state privacy statutes provide minors with privacy protection?

Some state privacy statutes are drafted broadly to encompass "all" patrons, while others explicitly apply to adults. Moreover, some statutes refer to "all" patrons, but specifically permit parents to gain access to the records of their minors. Lawyers representing libraries must be familiar with their state statute in order to assist the library in drafting a confidentiality policy that is compliant with state law. If your state statute does not specifically *exclude* minors, then the library confidentiality policy should apply to "all" patrons regardless of age.

Does case law distinguish between adults and minors in the privacy that will be accorded to patron use information?

Courts that have attempted to balance the First Amendment and privacy interests of citizens against the law enforcement interests of government officials attempting to gain access to information have not distinguished between adults and minors. Nonetheless, no court has squarely addressed this issue.

NOTES

1. *Tinker v. Des Moines Indep. Community Sch. Dist.*, 393 U.S. 503, 506 (1969).

2. *Id.* at 511.

3. *American Amusements Machine v. Kendrick*, 244 F.3d 572, 577 (7th Cir.), *cert. denied*, 534 U.S. 994 (2001).

4. *Board of Education v. Pico*, 457 U.S. at 871.

5. *Id.* at 864.

6. *Sund v. City of Wichita Falls*, 121 F. Supp. 2d 530 (N.D. Tex. 2000).

7. *Id.* at 549.

8. *Counts v. Cedarville School District*, 295 F. Supp. 2d 996 (W.D. Ark. 2003).

9. *Ginsberg v. New York*, 390 U.S. 629 (1968).

10. *FCC v. Pacifica Foundation*, 438 U.S. 726 (1978).

11. *Id.* at 749–50.

12. *See Sable Communications of California v. FCC*, 492 U.S. 115, 127–28 (1989); *Reno v. ACLU*, 521 U.S. 844, 864–65 (1997).

13. *See Erznoznik v. City of Jacksonville*, 422 U.S. 205, 212–14 (1975).

14. *American Booksellers Assn. v. Virginia*, 882 F.2d 125, 127 (4th Cir. 1989), *cert. denied*, 494 U.S. 1056 (1990); and *American Booksellers v. Webb*, 919 F.2d 1493, 1504–5 (11th Cir. 1990), *cert. denied*, 500 U.S. 942 (1991).

Chapter Six

FEDERAL LAWS

In addition to understanding how state law impacts the privacy rights of patrons, libraries must be aware of federal laws that govern confidentiality issues related to library use. This chapter provides an overview of current federal laws that have an impact on libraries.

What impact does federal law have on my library?

Federal law preempts state laws. In other words, if a federal law regulates a particular subject matter, then it will govern rather than state law. This preemption cuts both ways. In some instances, a federal law may provide more privacy protection than a state law. In other cases, however, federal law may offer law enforcement officials greater authority to secure access to private information. If there is a conflict, federal law controls.

Are there any federal laws that protect the privacy rights of patrons in the library?

The release of information related to video use is prohibited by the Video Privacy Protection Act. This law was enacted in 1988 after the video rental records of Robert Bork, a nominee for the Supreme Court, were publicly disseminated during his confirmation hearings. This statute applies in every state without regard to whether the individual state's confidentiality statute encompasses videos. Libraries must incorporate this protection into their privacy policies to the extent that they provide borrowing privileges for videos.

Can federal law enforcement ask my library for patron information?

Federal law enforcement officials may utilize any of the methods used by state investigators, such as informal requests, subpoenas, or search warrants. Additionally, federal law enforcement officers may make Patriot Act requests for information or issue a demand for information with a National Security Letter.

What are National Security Letters?

National Security Letters are administrative subpoenas used by the Federal Bureau of Investigation (FBI) to obtain several types of records. There is no judicial oversight of NSLs. They are issued directly by the FBI without judicial review. NSLs apply to "electronic communication transactional records" as well as financial records, credit card records, and consumer credit records. Patron Internet transaction records maintained by libraries are the type of electronic transaction records covered by the statute.

Does the ability to use National Security Letters expand the authority of federal officials to access private information?

National Security Letters predate the Patriot Act, but the FBI has conceded that the Patriot Act greatly increases its authority to access information: "The USA PATRIOT Act has greatly simplified the NSL process. The FBI official authorizing the issuance of an NSL is no longer required to certify that there are specific and articulable facts giving reason to believe that the information sought pertains to a foreign power, or an agent of a foreign power. NSLs may now be issued upon a certification of relevance to an authorized investigation to protect against international terrorism or clandestine intelligence activities" (FBI Memorandum, Nov. 28, 2001, at 7).

Can an NSL recipient challenge the request for information?

Yes. An NSL recipient may file a petition to modify or set aside the request in the federal district court in which the recipient or entity to which the request is directed resides or does business. The court will review the petition and may set aside the order if compliance would be "unreasonable, oppressive or otherwise unlawful." To date, no court has applied this standard and provided guidance on what type of request will be held "unreasonable, oppressive or otherwise unlawful." In an amicus brief in a case challenging the constitutionality of the NSL statute, organizations devoted to reader privacy issues argued that the government should be held to a high standard and that NSL requests should be set aside if the government cannot demonstrate that it has a compelling need for the information, a reasonable nexus exists between the request and the information sought, and there is no reasonable alternative means to locate the information. Because the actual request for information was withdrawn while the matter was pending, the court did not resolve the issue of which test should be applied to NSL challenges.

Will the public be permitted to attend an NSL challenge hearing?

The government may request that an NSL challenge be filed "under seal" and that the court's review be conducted *in camera* by the assigned judge. In other words, the request and the particulars of the challenge cannot be disclosed publicly and the judge will conduct the review without a public hearing. When complaints or challenges are filed "under seal," the public record of the filing will be redacted to delete the names of the parties, information related to the details of the request, and any information that might reveal the particulars of the government's request for information.

Do National Security Letters contain a gag order?

Yes. National Security Letters contain a nondisclosure order that, if unchallenged, is permanent and indefinite. NSLs can be disclosed only to two categories of people: (1) an attorney for purposes of seeking legal advice related to production of the items sought by the order, and (2) a person to whom disclosure is "necessary" to permit compliance with the order. If requested by the FBI, the recipient of the request for records must inform the FBI of the identity of the person to whom disclosure has been made, other than an attorney consulted for legal advice related to the order. The recipient also is obligated to inform any person to whom disclosure is made that the order is accompanied by a gag order requirement.

Can the recipient of an NSL request challenge the gag order?

The 2006 reauthorization provisions provide that a recipient can challenge an NSL gag order. If the challenge is filed within one year of the NSL request, the court will set aside the gag order if "there is no reason to believe that disclosure may endanger the national security of the United States, interfere with a criminal, counterterrorism, or counterintelligence investigation, interfere with diplomatic relations or endanger the life or physical safety of any person." Pursuant to the terms of the statute, however, the government retains broad authority to retain the gag order in place beyond the first year. Once a request to lift the gag order is made, government officials may certify that disclosure "may endanger the national security of the United States or interfere with diplomatic relations." If such a certification is made, the court must treat it as "conclusive" unless the court finds the certification was made in bad faith. The statute does not define what constitutes a "danger" to national security and thus leaves much to the discretion of the government officials. The statute also does not provide courts with guidance in ascertaining whether the government officials are engaged in bad faith.

What will the court do if an NSL recipient files a petition to lift a gag order after the initial certification by the government that release of the records poses a threat to national security?

If the petition to lift the gag order is filed more than one year after the request for records was made, then the gag order must be terminated unless the government recertifies that disclosure should not be permitted because it may endanger the national security of the United States or interfere with diplomatic relations. The recertification must be treated as "conclusive" unless the court finds it was made in bad faith.

Are there any penalties for failing to comply with an NSL?

Yes. Any recipient that fails to comply with an NSL request may be held in contempt of court. Penalties may include fines or incarceration for up to five years.

Can penalties be imposed for violating an NSL gag order?

Yes. If a recipient of an NSL (or a person to whom a disclosure has been made legally under the statute) violates the gag order "knowingly and willfully," the person violating the gag order will be subject to fines and imprisonment of no more than one year. If the violation of the gag order is "knowingly committed with the intent to obstruct an investigation or judicial proceeding," fines or imprisonment for up to five years may be imposed on the person violating the order.

What is the Patriot Act?

In response to the 9/11 terrorism attacks upon the United States, Congress enacted the Patriot Act as a means of increasing the security of the nation. Congress expanded the types of records to which law enforcement can gain access to "any tangible thing (including books, records, papers, documents, and other items) for an investigation to protect against international terrorism or clandestine intelligence activities, provided that such investigation of a United States person is not conducted solely upon the basis of activities protected by the [F]irst [A]mendment to the Constitution." The definition is broad enough to encompass various types of patron use records, such as computer records of a patron's loan history, written Internet use logs, or technologically stored data related to an Internet user's search history.

Does the Patriot Act expand the authority of federal officials to access private information?

Yes. The Patriot Act amendments dramatically increased federal law enforcement powers. Whereas federal law enforcement officers previously could only access information concerning actual terrorism suspects, they now can access information generally about persons plainly not considered to be suspects if they allege that the investigation is designed to "protect against international terrorism or clandestine intelligence activities." Additionally, federal law enforcement officers no longer need to allege "specific and articulable" facts to support the need for information.

Does a Patriot Act request come directly from the Federal Bureau of Investigation?

No. The FBI must apply to the Foreign Intelligence Surveillance Court (FISA court) for an order permitting its agents to gain access to the specified items.

What is the standard applied by the Foreign Intelligence Surveillance Court for reviewing FBI requests for Patriot Act orders?

Federal agents must demonstrate that they have "reasonable grounds" to believe that the requested information is "relevant" to an authorized investigation. Pursuant to the statute, items will be deemed "presumptively relevant" if the FBI states that the requested information pertains to a foreign agent, foreign power, activities of a suspected agent of a foreign power, or an individual that is known to be in contact with the subject of an investigation.

Will the FISA court allow FBI agents access to all documents in the possession of the party to whom the request is directed?

No. The FBI is required to describe the items sought with "sufficient particularity" to allow them to be identified for production. The FBI will not be permitted unfettered access to all documents in the possession of the party to whom the request is directed.

If a library receives a Patriot Act request, can it disclose the existence of the request to anyone?

The Patriot Act statute imposes a nondisclosure or gag order on the recipient of the request for information. The FISA order can be disclosed only to two categories of people: (1) an attorney for purposes of seeking legal advice related to production of the items sought by the order, and (2) a person to whom disclosure is "necessary" to permit compliance with the order. If requested by the FBI, the recipient of the request for records must inform the FBI of the identity of the person to whom disclosure has been made, other than an attorney consulted for legal advice related to the order. The recipient also is obligated to inform any person to whom disclosure is made that the order is accompanied by a gag order requirement.

Can the recipient of a FISA order challenge the request for information?

Yes. The reauthorization of the Patriot Act included several important amendments, including a provision that permits the recipient of a request for information to challenge either the request for records or the accompanying gag order. The challenge to the order must be made with the FISA court. Any challenge to a Patriot Act request must be filed "under seal" and the review will be conducted *in camera* by the assigned judge. In other words, the request and the particulars of the challenge cannot be disclosed publicly and the judge will conduct the review without a public hearing.

What standard will the FISA court apply in reviewing whether an order for information should be withdrawn?

The FISA court may set aside the order if it is "unlawful." The statute does not further define when an order should be deemed "unlawful" by the FISA court. To date, there has been no further guidance from the FISA court or other legal opinion as to the definition of "unlawful."

Can the recipient of a Patriot Act request challenge the gag order?

The 2006 reauthorization provisions provide that a recipient can challenge a Patriot Act gag order one year after its receipt. Pursuant to the terms of the statute, however, the government retains broad authority to retain the secrecy of the information. If the government asserts that disclosure of the contents of the Patriot Act request would damage national security, then the FISA court will treat that claim as "conclusive" and the gag order will remain in place indefinitely.

What are the consequences of defying the Patriot Act request or gag order?

Although the Patriot Act amendments do not specify particular consequences for failure to comply with the request or the gag order, defying either the request or gag order could lead to general charges that the librarian obstructed justice.

Do the statutes provide First Amendment protection?

Both the Patriot Act statute and the amendments to the NSL provisions contain a limitation prohibiting the issuance of an NSL in an investigation of a "United States person" conducted "*solely* upon the basis of activities protected by the [F]irst [A]mendment to the Constitution."[1] The definition of a "United States person" includes a U.S. citizen, a permanent resident alien, an association with a substantial number of citizens or lawful permanent residents, or a corporation incorporated in the United States.[2] This reference to the First Amendment does not provide enough protection for First Amendment rights for two reasons: (1) the First Amendment protection does not cover investigations of third parties to which the records of a United States person may be relevant, and thus the provision does not protect the records of a library patron who is a United States citizen if the records being sought are connected to the FBI's investigation of a noncitizen; and (2) the First Amendment protection does not cover investigations of United States persons that are conducted *partially*, though not *solely*, on the basis of First Amendment–protected activity. The statute thus would appear to apply to situations where the FBI has information from another source regarding a United States person so that the patron's reading habits arguably are not the *sole* basis for the investigation.

If a library director or librarian receives a Patriot Act request or NSL, can he discuss it with his library board?

This is an issue that has not been resolved. With the exception of legal counsel, Patriot Act or NSL requests for information may only be disclosed to those persons "necessary" to compliance with the request. Whether disclosure can be made to the library board may depend to a large extent on how the library board is constituted and the range of its powers as juxtaposed with the authority provided to the library director. If, for example, the library director generally does not have the authority to produce documents without board approval, then one could argue that disclosure to the board is necessary. If, on the other hand, the library director enjoys broad authority to act on behalf of the library, then it would be much more difficult to argue that disclosure to the board was "necessary."

If a library director or librarian receives a Patriot Act request or NSL, can she call the local newspaper to discuss it or inform the target of the request that federal law enforcement officers are searching for information?

Library personnel are absolutely prohibited from discussing either the contents or the existence of a Patriot Act request or NSL with any member of the public, including the press, unless the gag order has been lifted.

Have there been any constitutional challenges to these new federal law enforcement tools?

Several cases have been filed challenging the expansion of the Patriot Act and NSLs on constitutional grounds. There are two types of constitutional challenges to statutes: facial challenges and as-applied challenges. A facial constitutional challenge to a statute alleges that the statute is so defective that it cannot be applied in a constitutional manner in any circumstance. This type of challenge may be asserted even if the government has made no effort to enforce or apply a statute. An as-applied challenge alleges that the statute has been applied in an unconstitutional manner in a particular circumstance.

Have any cases been filed alleging that the NSL provisions of the Patriot Act are unconstitutional?

Yes. Two cases have been filed alleging that the NSL provisions are unconstitutional. One case related to an NSL issued to an Internet service provider in New York, and the other case related to an NSL issued to a library consortium in Connecticut.

Who filed the constitutional challenge to the New York NSL?

In April 2004 the ACLU filed a challenge in federal court in the Southern District of New York challenging the use by the federal government of National Security Letters on behalf of an anonymous NSL recipient. The case was filed under seal and most of the pleadings in the case remained under seal. The judge ordered, however, that pleadings and information related to the facial challenge to the use of National Security Letters should be made public. In other words, the judge held that information related to whether NSLs could ever be applied in a constitutional manner (the facial challenge) could be litigated publicly. Information related to whether the particular NSL directed to this particular plaintiff was constitutional (the as-applied challenge) would remain under seal.

How did the court resolve the NSL challenge filed by the Internet service provider in New York?

On September 29, 2004, the district court granted the plaintiffs' motion for summary judgment, holding that the statute authorizing use of NSLs was unconstitutional because it did not include a process of judicial review and the permanent ban on disclosure operated as an unconstitutional prior restraint.[3]

Why did the New York court find the statute lacked a means for judicial review if the court was conducting a judicial review?

The district court specifically held that the statutory language provided no means of judicial review and the procedures utilized by the FBI in serving the NSLs had the practical effect of intimidating recipients into not seeking judicial review. The court identified the following actions as coercive: (1) a personal phone call from an FBI agent prior to service of the NSL; (2) the NSL request framed in imposing language referring to terrorist activities and on FBI letterhead; and (3) the order to provide disclosure in person and in complete secrecy. The district court concluded that the failure of the statute to provide an explicit mechanism for judicial review violated the Fourth Amendment of the Constitution.

The district court also considered the First Amendment implications of NSLs, concluding:

> The Court re-emphasizes that it does not here purport to set forth the scope of these First Amendment rights in general, or define them in this or any other case. The Court holds only that such fundamental rights are certainly implicated in some cases in which the Government may employ § 2709 broadly to gather information, thus requiring that the process incorporate the safeguards of some judicial review to ensure that if an infringement of those rights is asserted, they are adequately protected through fair process in an independent neutral tribunal. Because the necessary procedural protections are wholly absent here, the Court finds on this ground additional cause for invalidating § 2709 as applied.[4]

Did the court in New York find the gag order was unconstitutional?

The district court also held that the NSL statute was unconstitutional for mandating nondisclosure permanently and in every situation. Recognizing that the government has a compelling interest in fighting terrorism and that predicting when a disclosure of information might implicate national security concerns is difficult for a court inexperienced in national security matters, the district court acknowledged that "the Government should be accorded a due measure of deference when it asserts that secrecy is necessary for national security purposes in a *particular situation* involving *particular persons* at a *particular time*."[5] The district court held, however, that Section 2709 was unconstitutional for imposing "perpetual secrecy upon an entire category of future cases whose details are unknown and whose particular twists and turns may not justify, for all time and all places, demanding unremitting concealment and imposing a disproportionate burden on free speech."[6]

How did the government defend itself against the constitutional challenge in the New York NSL case?

In appealing the decision to the Second Circuit, the government took the position that (1) the statute does not prohibit seeking judicial review and does not coerce any recipient into forgoing judicial review; and (2) the secrecy requirement is necessary to protect current investigations and to protect against terrorists knowing how the FBI engages in investigations and information gathering. The appellate court remanded or sent the matter back to the district court because Congress amended the NSL statute while the appeal was pending.

What happened when the case was remanded?

On August 7, 2006, the ACLU filed an amended complaint arguing that the NSL statute was unconstitutional and the particular request for records was unlawful. The ACLU raised a number of issues, including: (1) that amendments to the gag rule do not cure the unconstitutionality of that provision because it remains essentially unreviewable, given that the government can keep the gag order in place simply by certifying that it is necessary, a finding that the reviewing court must accept as "conclusive" unless there is evidence of "bad faith"; (2) although the new amendments to the statute permit an NSL recipient to challenge the NSL in court, the provision remains unconstitutional because the government can demand an *ex parte* proceeding making it difficult to challenge the NSL and preventing the public from monitoring the government's use of NSLs; and (3) the request itself, issued on the basis that the information is needed to "protect against international terrorism or clandestine intelligence activities," is insufficient when balanced against the important First Amendment rights at stake rendering it "unlawful" unless the government could show that its need for the information was compelling, the request was narrowly tailored to secure the information, and there are no alternative sources from which the government could secure the information without implicating First Amendment rights.

How did the district court resolve the issues on remand?

On November 22, 2006, the FBI withdrew its demand for records but kept in place the nondisclosure order directed to John Doe. In September 2007 the district court once again concluded that the NSL statute was unconstitutional. The court held that the statute was unconstitutional for two reasons: (1) the government's use of gag orders "must be narrowly tailored on a case-by-case basis" and "may not be broader in either scope or duration than the degree of secrecy required to serve the government's interest in protecting national security"; and (2) the gag orders must be subject to "meaningful judicial review," and Congress cannot supersede the authority of the court to apply "the standard of review the judge determines is mandated by constitutional law" rather than "an overly deferential standard imposed by Congress." In sum, therefore, the court held that the NSL statute cannot impose a gag order in every instance without a particular analysis of whether the order was required in that particular case. The court also held that the statute usurps the authority of the courts by mandating that judges accept the government's claim that the nondisclosure order should continue as "conclusive."[7]

Who filed the challenge to an NSL in Connecticut?

A member of the American Library Association in Connecticut was served with a National Security Letter seeking patron information. The ACLU filed a complaint in federal district court in Connecticut arguing that the provisions of the NSL are unconstitutional, including the gag requirement that prohibits the recipient of the NSL from disclosing receipt of the NSL. Because the gag order was in place, the complaint was filed under seal and basic facts about the matter were not publicly available, including the identity of the recipient and the records that were sought through the NSL. The ACLU urged the court to lift the gag order while the merits of the NSL request were pending.

How did the court resolve the NSL challenge filed by the Connecticut library consortium?

On September 20, 2005, Judge Hall of the U.S. District Court in Connecticut, after reviewing the briefs on the matter and an *ex parte* review of classified material, agreed with the ACLU that the gag order should be lifted. The district court held that the recipient of the NSL would suffer irreparable harm in not being permitted to participate publicly in the debate regarding the renewal of the federal Patriot Act. Additionally, the district court held that in the particular circumstances of this case, the government had failed to demonstrate that disclosing the identity of the recipient of the NSL would harm any particular national security investigation or national security investigations generally. Finally, the district court held that the permanent gag order was not narrowly tailored to serve a compelling interest because every investigation—even if it might last longer in the context of a national security matter—would end eventually and a gag order could serve no useful purpose at that point.[8]

Was the Connecticut NSL case appealed?

Yes. The district court granted the government's request for a stay pending an expedited appeal of the order to the Second Circuit. The government appealed and the matter was further stayed by the appellate court. The ACLU filed an emergency application to the Supreme Court requesting a lifting of the stay, but that application was denied. The case was consolidated with the NSL matter from the Southern District of New York and both cases were argued on November 2, 2005. While the case was pending, the NSL statute was amended and the government unilaterally decided that the recipient of the National Security Letter in Connecticut was free to disclose its identity. Thus, the appellate court held that the appeal should be dismissed on mootness grounds. When the case was remanded, the government decided to withdraw the request for information and the case was dismissed.

Who filed the challenge to the Patriot Act?

In July 2003 the ACLU filed a challenge to Section 215 of the Patriot Act in federal district court in Michigan. The ACLU complaint alleged that the federal statute is facially unconstitutional because it violates the free speech, privacy, and due process rights of citizens. The ACLU complaint focused on several factors: (1) the statute can be used to obtain information about people plainly not involved in any criminal activity because the FBI need only certify that the records are "sought for" a foreign intelligence, clandestine intelligence, or international terrorism investigation; (2) the FISA court that issues the order has no authority to examine the underlying basis for the FBI's request; (3) there is no procedure in the statute for challenging a specific FISA order prior to producing the requested documents; and (4) the statute provides for a gag order in every request for an indefinite time and without any particular showing by the FBI that a gag order is necessary.

On what grounds did the government defend the constitutionality of the Patriot Act?

The government moved to dismiss the complaint for several reasons: (1) that the plaintiffs have no standing to challenge the statute because they have not suffered any "actual harm" in that Section 215 has never been used; (2) there is nothing that prevents an entity served with a subpoena from filing an objection with the FISA court objecting to the request; (3) there is no explicit requirement under the Fourth Amendment that requires a showing of probable cause before a court may order production of documents; and (4) there is no due process right of notice to the "target" of an investigation before the government may obtain production of documents.

How was the Patriot Act case resolved?

The ACLU withdrew the challenge to the Patriot Act after the amendments to the statute in 2006 but confirmed that it would continue to monitor the FBI's use of Patriot Act requests to the extent possible given the secrecy provisions associated with these types of requests.

Is there any oversight of the FBI's use of Patriot Act requests?

Yes. The amendments to the Patriot Act in 2006 added two types of oversight: (1) the attorney general must provide a report to Congress on an annual, rather than semiannual, basis in "unclassified" form and must include the total number of applications made by the government to the FISA court as well as the total number of orders granted, modified, or denied; and (2) the inspector general must perform a "comprehensive" audit of the "effectiveness and use, including any improper or illegal use, of the investigative authority" provided to the FBI under FISA, determining whether the minimization procedures protect the constitutional rights of United States citizens and the extent to which information produced pursuant to a FISA order was used by the FBI in its operations or used in a criminal proceeding. The report must be presented in an unclassified format but may include a classified index.

Is there any oversight of the FBI's use of NSL requests?

Yes. The amendments to the Patriot Act in 2006 added two types of oversight to the NSL provisions: (1) the attorney general must provide a report to Congress each April with an "aggregate" report specifying the total number of requests by the Department of Justice in the preceding year in an unclassified form; and (2) the inspector general must perform a "comprehensive" audit of the "effectiveness and use, including any improper or illegal use, of the investigative authority" provided to the government through the use of NSLs. Among other things, the inspector general must determine whether the minimization procedures protect the constitutional rights of United States citizens and the extent to which information produced pursuant to NSLs was used for analytical purposes or in a criminal proceeding. The report must be presented in an unclassified format but may include a classified index.

NOTES

1. Electronic Communications Privacy Act, codified at 18 U.S.C. § 2709(b)(1), *id.* § 2709(b)(2) (2006).

2. 50 U.S.C. § 1801(i) (2000).

3. *Ashcroft v. Gonzales*, 334 F. Supp. 2d 471 (S.D.N.Y. 2004), *vacated and remanded by*, 449 F.3d 415 (2d Cir. 2006).

4. *Id.*

5. *Id.* (emphasis in text).

6. *Id.*

7. *Doe v. Gonzales*, 500 F. Supp. 2d 471 (S.D.N.Y. 2007) (appeal pending).

8. *Doe v. Gonzales*, 386 F. Supp. 2d 66 (D. Conn. 2005), *dismissed as moot by*, 449 F. 3d 415 (2d Cir. 2006).

Chapter Seven

DEVELOPING PRIVACY POLICIES

Should libraries have privacy and confidentiality policies?

Yes. Libraries that have privacy and confidentiality policies are better equipped to address issues that arise in the library. Existing policies form the basis for asserting that important First Amendment rights are at stake and that patrons have an expectation of privacy in the library.

Who should develop a privacy policy?

Library staff should work with their legal counsel to develop a privacy policy for use of the library and library materials.

What aspects of library use should be covered by a privacy policy?

Every aspect of library use should be covered by the privacy policy, including circulation of materials, use of the Internet, processing of hold requests, and use of the library facility.

Is training staff important?

Training of staff is critical. A trained staff will know exactly how to react when confidentiality issues arise. For example, staff should be trained in how to respond to a request for information about a patron that may be transmitted from a law enforcement officer to the library assistant at the checkout desk. Staff must be trained to respond to complaints about Internet use. Staff should be instructed in the method by which holds are stored and processed for patrons.

How should the library privacy policy apply to materials placed on hold?

The library must ensure that its hold policy does not encroach upon the privacy of patrons. For example, if the library places hold materials on an open shelf for patrons to peruse the materials to find their own hold requests, the library should consider using a wrapper that would cover the title of the work. Otherwise, other patrons will be able to discover what materials are being requested by particular patrons.

Do surveillance cameras and tapes raise privacy concerns?

Surveillance cameras raise privacy concerns that should be addressed by the library as it determines whether to implement their use. Surveillance cameras may be necessary to address issues of patron security, theft, or vandalism. The placement of such surveillance cameras, however, should be carefully considered. To the greatest extent possible, the cameras must be used in a manner that detects criminal violations without revealing the particular materials being used or borrowed by patrons. Additionally, the library should carefully consider how long it retains surveillance tapes. Tapes should not be retained longer than necessary to assist with security issues.

Should the library have a document retention and destruction policy?

Yes. Every library should have a document retention and destruction policy. Documentation regarding patron use and circulation of materials should be kept only as long as necessary to assist with the administration of the library. The library should consider whether it needs to keep circulation records once the material has been returned by the patron and the record is not needed for overdue notices. Similarly, the library should consider whether it needs to keep Internet log-in information once the patron's session is completed. If any records are not needed to assist staff with the administration of the library, then there is no reason to retain them. Library staff should consult with legal counsel to determine whether any current federal, state, or local laws impose any particular obligations to retain documents.

Once a library receives a request for information from law enforcement personnel, should any document destruction plan be suspended?

Yes. Once a request for information has been made by a law enforcement officer, the library should suspend any document destruction policy until the issue of whether the materials must be produced has been evaluated by counsel and resolved by a court.

Where does a library start in creating a privacy and confidentiality policy?

There are many examples of library confidentiality policies available from other libraries. The Office for Intellectual Freedom of the American Library Association can also assist libraries with examples of confidentiality policies. Each library should, however, consult its own attorney to ensure that the policy developed for that particular library comports with federal and state laws and is the policy that is best suited to that particular library.

Should libraries conduct a privacy audit?

Yes. Periodically, every library—even one with a confidentiality policy in place—should conduct an audit of its facility and administration to ensure that the policy in place is being administered correctly and to determine whether any changes are necessary to address new programs or needs of patrons.

STATE PRIVACY AND CONFIDENTIALITY STATUTES

NOTE

This state survey, compiled in September 2008, is designed to guide the librarian or lawyer quickly to the right place to look for the current law in their state when confronted by a request for library patron records. The restatement of the law in this text should serve merely as a guide to further legal research for two reasons: (1) laws are amended constantly and the language may have changed since this printing; and (2) this survey contains only pertinent excerpts from the statutes and not the full reprint of the law and accompanying relevant provisions. **The researcher must determine if the legal language appearing here is still in effect at the time of the particular request for records and must review the entire statute to determine the precise law applicable to library patron records.** This survey is designed merely to serve as a starting point for further research.

ALABAMA

The Alabama state legislature has recognized that an individual's use of the public library should be considered of a "confidential nature." Specifically, state law provides that "the registration and circulation records and information concerning the use of the public, public school, college and university libraries of this state shall be confidential" and cannot be "open for inspection by, or otherwise available to, any agency or individual except for the following entities: (a) the library which manages the records; (b) the state education department for a library under its jurisdiction when it is necessary to assure the proper operation of such library; or (c) the state Public Library Service for a library under its jurisdiction when it is necessary to assure the proper operations of such library." Libraries may, however, release "[a]ggregate statistics shown from registration and circulation records, with all personal identification removed," if needed by the library for "research and planning purposes." The Alabama state legislation also creates a specific exception for parents seeking to access the records of their minors: "any parent of a minor child shall have the right to inspect the registration and circulation records of any school or public library that pertain to his or her child." ALA. CODE § 41-8-10 (2008).

ALASKA

The Alaska state legislature has mandated that "the names, addresses, or other personal identifying information of people who have used materials made available to the public by a library shall be kept confidential" and may only be released pursuant to a "court order." The confidentiality mandate "applies to libraries operated by the state, a municipality, or a public school, including the University of Alaska." The legislature did, however, create an exception for parents seeking the school library records of their minor children: "Records of a public elementary or secondary school library identifying a minor child shall be made available on request to a parent or guardian of that child." ALASKA STAT. § 40.25.140 (2008).

ARIZONA

The Arizona state legislature has mandated that "a library or library system supported by public monies shall not allow disclosure of any record or other information which identifies a user of library services as requesting or obtaining specific materials or services or as otherwise using the library." Arizona law provides that library records may be disclosed only in limited circumstances: (1) where necessary for the reasonable operation of the library; (2) upon written consent of the user; (3) pursuant to a court order; and (4) where required by law. Arizona law explicitly criminalizes the intentional disclosure of confidential library records: "Any person who knowingly discloses any record or other information in violation of this section is guilty of a class 3 misdemeanor." ARIZ. REV. STAT. § 41-1354 (2008).

ARKANSAS

The Arkansas state legislature has mandated that "[l]ibrary records which contain names or other personally identifying details regarding the patrons of public, school, academic, and special libraries and library systems supported in whole or in part by public funds shall be confidential." The state legislature defines "confidential library records" expansively as "documents or information in any format retained in a library that identify a patron as having requested, used, or obtained specific materials, including, but not limited to, circulation of library books, materials, computer database searches, interlibrary loan transactions, reference queries, patent searches, requests for photocopies of library materials, title reserve requests, or the use of audiovisual materials, films, or records." Disclosure is permitted to the patron, pursuant to a court order or in situations where the patron consents to the production of records. The library also may disclose patron information to "[a]ny person, including, but not limited to, the patron, who has received an automated telephone notification or other electronic communication for overdue materials or reserve materials if the person making the request can verify the telephone number or e-mail address to which the notice was sent." Otherwise, Arkansas law provides that any person who "knowingly" releases confidential library records "shall be guilty of a misdemeanor and shall be punished by a fine of not more than two hundred dollars ($200) or thirty (30) days in jail, or both, or a sentence of appropriate public service or education, or both." Additionally, Arkansas statutes provide that public libraries must use "an automated or Gaylord-type circulation system that does not identify a patron with circulated materials after materials are returned." ARK. CODE ANN. §§ 13-2-701 through 13-2-704 (2008).

CALIFORNIA

California law provides that "[a]ll registration and circulation records of any library which is in whole or in part supported by public funds shall remain confidential and shall not be disclosed to any person, local agency, or state agency" with only three limited exceptions: (a) by a person acting within the scope of his or her duties within the administration of the library; (b) by a person authorized, in writing, by the individual to whom the records pertain, to inspect the records; and (c) by order of the appropriate superior court. The definition of "registration records" is broad and includes "any information which a library requires a patron to provide in order to become eligible to borrow books and other materials," while "circulation records" are defined as "any information which identifies the patrons borrowing particular books and other material." The California statute specifically permits the public release of "statistical reports of registration and circulation" and "records of fines collected by the library." CAL. GOV'T. CODE § 6267 (2007).

COLORADO

The Colorado state legislature has mandated that "a publicly-supported library shall not disclose any record or other information that identifies a person as having requested or obtained specific materials or service or as otherwise having used the library." Disclosure of library patron records is permitted only in limited circumstances: (a) when necessary for the reasonable operation of the library; (b) upon written consent of the user; (c) pursuant to subpoena, upon court order, or where otherwise required by law; and (d) to a custodial parent or legal guardian who has access to a minor's library card or its authorization number for the purpose of accessing by electronic means library records of the minor. Violation of this statute by any "library official, employee, or volunteer" constitutes a "class 2 petty offense and, upon conviction thereof, shall be punished by a fine of not more than three hundred dollars." COLO. REV. STAT. § 24-90-119 (2008).

CONNECTICUT

Connecticut state law provides that any "personally identifiable information contained in the circulation records of all public libraries shall be confidential." CONN. GEN. STAT. ANN. § 11-25 (2008).

DELAWARE

Delaware law defines a "public record" as "information of any kind, owned, made, used, retained, received, produced, composed, drafted or otherwise compiled or collected, by any public body, relating in any way to public business, or in any way of public interest, or in any way related to public purposes, regardless of the physical form or characteristic by which such information is stored, recorded or reproduced," but provides explicitly that "[a]ny records of a public library which contain the identity of a user and the books, documents, films, recordings or other property of the library which a patron has used" are not considered "public records." DEL. CODE ANN., tit. 29, § 10002 (2007).

DISTRICT OF COLUMBIA

District of Columbia law provides that "[c]irculation records maintained by the public library in the District of Columbia which can be used to identify a library patron who has requested, used, or borrowed identified library materials from the public library and the specific material that patron has requested, used, or borrowed from the public library, shall be kept confidential, except that the records may be disclosed to officers, employees, and agents of the public library to the extent necessary for the proper operation of the public library." The law also provides that circulation records may be disclosed "with the written permission of the affected library patron or as the result of a court order."

District of Columbia law also sets forth a specific procedure for challenging requests for disclosure of confidential library records. The law explicitly provides that a person whose records are sought "may file a motion in the Superior Court of the District of Columbia requesting that the records be kept confidential . . . accompanied by the reasons for the request." To facilitate a challenge by the person whose records have been requested, the law requires the library to send a copy of the subpoena by certified mail within two working days of receipt to the subject of the request with the following notice: "Records or information concerning your borrowing records in the public library in the District of Columbia are being sought pursuant to the enclosed subpoena. In accordance with the District of Columbia Confidentiality of Library Records Act of 1984, these records will not be released until 10 days from the date this notice was mailed. If you desire that these records or information not be released, you must file a motion in the Superior Court of the District of Columbia requesting that the records be kept confidential, and state your reasons for the request. A sample motion is enclosed. You may wish to contact a lawyer. If you do not have a lawyer, you may call the District of Columbia Bar Lawyer Referral Service." This notice may be waived only by court order if the presiding judge finds that "(A) the investigation being conducted is within the lawful jurisdiction of the government authority seeking the records; (B) there is reason to believe that the records being sought are relevant to a legitimate law enforcement inquiry; or (C) there is reason to believe that the notice will result in: (i) endangering the life or physical safety of any person; (ii) flight from prosecution; (iii) destruction of or tampering with evidence; (iv) intimidation of potential witnesses; or (v) otherwise seriously jeopardizing an investigation or official proceeding."

District of Columbia law also provides that "any officer, employee, or agent of the public library who shall violate any provision of this section or any rules issued pursuant to it commits a misdemeanor, and upon conviction shall be punished by a fine of not more than $300. The aggrieved public library patron may also bring a civil action against the individual violator for actual damages or $250, whichever is greater, reasonable attorneys' fees, and court costs." D.C. CODE ANN. § 39-108 (2008).

FLORIDA

The Florida legislature has mandated that "[a]ll registration and circulation records of every public library, except statistical reports of registration and circulation, are confidential" and may not be disclosed in the absence of "a proper judicial order." Additionally, the library or any agent of the library may disclose registration and circulation records "for the purpose of collecting fines or recovering overdue books, documents, films, or other items or materials owned or otherwise belonging to the library" to the following persons or entities: (1) the library patron named in the records; (2) the parent or guardian of any patron less than 16 years of age; (3) any entity that collects fines on behalf of a library if the patron is more than 16 years old or the identifying information of the parent or guardian if the patron is less than

16 years of age; (4) municipal or county law enforcement officials for patrons over the age of 16 or their parents if the patron is 16 years old; and (5) judicial officials. The Florida statute also provides that violation of the disclosure provisions constitutes "a misdemeanor of the second degree." FLA. STAT. ANN. § 257.261 (2008).

GEORGIA

Georgia law provides that "[c]irculation and similar records of a library which identify the user of library materials shall not be public records" and may only be disclosed in limited circumstances: (1) to library staff in the ordinary course of business; (2) with written consent of the user of the library materials or the user's parents or guardian if the user is a minor or ward; or (3) pursuant to an appropriate court order or subpoena. GA. CODE ANN. § 24-9-46 (2008).

HAWAII

The state legislature in Hawaii has mandated that information may not be disclosed publicly if to do so constitutes a "clearly unwarranted invasion of personal privacy" (HAW. REV. STAT. § 92F-2 [2008]). The attorney general of Hawaii has issued an opinion letter stating in pertinent part that "individuals have a significant privacy interest in information, such as Library circulation records, which reveals their thoughts, associations, or beliefs" and that "generally, the public disclosure of Library circulation records would 'constitute a clearly unwarranted invasion of personal privacy' under the UIPA" (OIP Opinion Letter No. 90-30 [Oct. 23, 1990] [Hugh R. Jones, Staff Attorney, Attorney General's Office to the Honorable Bartholomew A. Kane, State Librarian]). With respect to fines for overdue materials, the office of the attorney general concluded that "although individuals may have a significant privacy interest in information concerning fines assessed against them by the Library, the public interest in the disclosure of this information outweighs the privacy interests of the individual" and "[a]ccordingly, we conclude that the disclosure of information regarding library fines that have been assessed or collected from individuals would not result in a clearly unwarranted invasion of personal privacy under the UIPA" (*id.*).

IDAHO

The Idaho state legislature has mandated that the "records of a library which, when examined alone, or when examined with other public records, would reveal the identity of the library patron checking out, requesting, or using an item from a library" are exempt from disclosure. IDAHO CODE § 9-340E(3) (2008).

ILLINOIS

Illinois law provides that the "registration and circulation records of a library are confidential information." Registration and circulation records may only be disclosed pursuant to a court order or if "the information is requested by a sworn law enforcement officer who represents that it is impractical to secure a court order as a result of an emergency where the law enforcement officer has probable cause to believe that there is an imminent danger of physical harm." If information is requested by a law enforcement officer on the grounds of exigent circumstances, the "information requested must be limited to identifying a suspect, witness, or victim of a crime" and the information requested without a court order "may not include the disclosure of registration or circulation records that would indicate materials borrowed, resources reviewed, or services used at the library." The statute provides further that "[i]f requested to do so by the library, the requesting law enforcement officer must sign a form acknowledging the receipt of the information" and that a "library providing the information may seek subsequent judicial review to assess compliance with this Section."

The statute defines "library" as "any public library or library of an educational, historical or eleemosynary institution, organization or society." The term "registration records" includes "any information a library requires a person to provide in order for that person to become eligible to borrow books and other materials." The term "circulation records" includes "all information identifying the individual borrowing particular books or materials." 75 I.L.C.S. § 70/1 (2008).

INDIANA

Indiana law provides that certain public records may be withheld from disclosure "at the discretion of a public agency." Included on that list are "library or archival records" that "can be used to identify any library patron." Additionally, the statute provides that a public agency may withhold from disclosure library or archival records that are "deposited with or acquired by a library upon a condition that the records be disclosed only: (i) to qualified researchers; (ii) after the passing of a period of years that is specified in the documents under which the deposit or acquisition is made; or (iii) after the death of persons specified at the time of the acquisition or deposit." IND. CODE ANN. § 5-14-3-4 (2008).

IOWA

The Iowa state legislature has mandated that certain public records "shall be kept confidential, unless otherwise ordered by a court, by the lawful custodian of the records, or by another person duly authorized to release such information." The list of protected records includes the "records of a library which, by themselves or when examined with other public records, would reveal the identity of the library patron checking out or requesting an item or information from the library." With respect to library patron records, the statute provides further that the "records shall be released to a criminal or juvenile justice agency only pursuant to an investigation of a particular person or organization suspected of committing a known crime" and may only be released "upon a judicial determination that a rational connection exists between the requested release of information and a legitimate end and that the need for the information is cogent and compelling." IOWA CODE § 22.7 (2008).

KANSAS

The Kansas legislature has mandated that "[e]xcept to the extent disclosure is otherwise required by law," public agencies are not required to disclose a number of public records, including "[l]ibrary patron and circulation records which pertain to identifiable individuals." KAN. STAT. ANN. § 45-221 (2007).

KENTUCKY

The state of Kentucky does not provide statutory protection for library patron records. Two attorney general opinions, however, advise that libraries may refuse to disclose library circulation records. In 1981, the attorney general issued the following opinion: "You have requested an opinion of the Attorney General as to whether records of public libraries are mandatorily required to be open to the public under the Open Records Law . . . [and] [i]t is our opinion that they are not" (OAG 81-159 [April 21, 1981] [Opinion by Steven L. Beshear, Attorney General, and Carl Miller, Assistant Attorney General to Mr. James A. Nelson, State Librarian and Commissioner]). The advisory opinion states further that "[w]e think that the individual's privacy rights as to what he borrows from a public library (books, motion picture film, periodicals and any other matter) is overwhelming" and "[i]n fact we can see no public interest at all to put in the scales opposite the privacy rights of the individual" (*id.*). The attorney general noted, however, that "Kentucky has no privacy statute and that the exceptions to mandatory disclosure of public records are permissive and no law is violated if they are not observed by the custodian" (*id.*). The attorney general opinion stated in summary that "it is our opinion that the custodian of the registration and circulation records of a public library is not required to make such records available for public inspection under the Open Records Law" (*id.*).

In 1982, the attorney general reiterated that "all libraries may refuse to disclose for public inspection their circulation records" (OAG 82-149 [March 12, 1982] [Opinion by Steven L. Beshear, Attorney General, and Carl Miller, Assistant Attorney General to Mr. James A. Nelson, State Librarian and Commissioner]). The advisory opinion states further that "[a]s far as the Open Records Law is concerned, they may also make the records open if they so choose; however, we believe that the privacy rights which are inherent in a democratic society should constrain all libraries to keep their circulation lists confidential" (*id.*).

LOUISIANA

The Louisiana state legislature has mandated that "records of any library which is in whole or in part supported by public funds, including the records of public, academic, school, and special libraries, and the State Library of Louisiana, indicating which of its documents or other materials, regardless of format, have been loaned to or used by an identifiable individual or group of individuals may not be disclosed except to a parent or custodian of a minor child seeking access to that child's records, to persons acting within the scope of their duties in the administration of the library, to persons authorized in writing by the individual or group of individuals to inspect such records, or by order of a court of law." The statute provides, however, that "[n]o provision of this Section shall be so construed as to prohibit or hinder any library or any business office operating jointly with a library from collecting overdue books, documents, films, or other items and/or materials owned or otherwise belonging to such library, nor shall any provision of this Section be so construed as to prohibit or hinder any such library or business office from collecting fines on such overdue books, documents, films, or other items and/or materials." Moreover, the statute provides that "[n]o provision of this section shall be so construed as to prohibit or hinder any library or librarian from providing information to appropriate law enforcement officers investigating criminal activity in the library witnessed by an employee or patron of the library and reported by the administrative librarian to the appropriate law enforcement officials." The statute defines "criminal activity" as a crime occurring in a library building, on library property, or "near a library and the proximity of such activity to a library or library property constitutes an element of the offense." The statute clarifies that the "information" that may be disclosed in a criminal investigation "shall include but not be limited to electronic data files, security surveillance video tapes, or other records or materials which may constitute evidence which would assist law enforcement officers in identifying the individual or group of individuals who may have committed criminal activity in the library." LA. REV. STAT. § 44:13 (2007).

MAINE

The Maine legislature has mandated that "[r]ecords maintained by any public municipal library, the Maine State Library, the Law and Legislative Reference Library and libraries of the University of Maine System and the Maine Maritime Academy that contain information relating to the identity of a library patron relative to the patron's use of books or other materials at the library are confidential." The statute provides further that library records "may only be released with the express written permission of the patron involved or as the result of a court order." ME. REV. STAT. ANN. tit. 27, § 121 (2007).

MARYLAND

Maryland law provides that "circulation records" of a public library, free association, school, college, or university library shall not be disclosed if the record "(i) is maintained by a library; (ii) contains an individual's name or the identifying number, symbol, or other identifying particular assigned to the individual; and (iii) identifies the use a patron makes of that library's materials, services, or facilities." The custodian of the records "shall permit inspection, use, or disclosure of a circulation record of a public library only in connection with the library's ordinary business and only for the purposes for which the record was created." MD. STATE GOV'T CODE ANN. § 10-616 (2007) (public library provision); MD. EDUC. CODE ANN. § 23-107 (2007) (school library provision).

MASSACHUSETTS

The Massachusetts legislature has mandated that "records of a public library which reveal the identity and intellectual pursuits of a person using such library shall not be a public record" but that libraries "may disclose or exchange information relating to library users for the purposes of inter-library cooperation and coordination, including but not limited to, the purposes of facilitating the sharing of resources among library jurisdictions." MASS. GEN. LAWS ANN., ch. 78, § 7 (2008).

MICHIGAN

The Michigan legislature has mandated that, with limited exceptions, "a library record is not subject to the disclosure requirements of the freedom of information act." A library may produce the records of a patron if "ordered by a court after giving the affected library notice of the request and an opportunity to be heard on the request" or after receipt of "written consent of the person liable for payment for or return of the materials identified in that library record." The statute provides further that the "procedure and form" of the written consent "may be determined by the library" and that a "a library may appear and be represented by counsel at a hearing" scheduled by the court for determining whether materials should be disclosed. Moreover, the state legislature has provided that a library employee or agent that improperly releases patron library records "shall be liable to the person identified in a record that is improperly released or disclosed" and the person whose records have been disclosed "may bring a civil action for actual damages or $250.00, whichever is greater; reasonable attorney fees; and the costs of bringing the action." MICH. COMP. LAWS §§ 397.603, 397.604 (2008).

MINNESOTA

The Minnesota state legislature has mandated that "the following data maintained by a library are private data on individuals and may not be disclosed for other than library purposes except pursuant to a court order: (1) data that link a library patron's name with materials requested or borrowed by the patron or that link a patron's name with a specific subject about which the patron has requested information or materials; or (2) data in applications for borrower cards, other than the name of the borrower." The statute does provide, however, that a "library may release reserved materials to a family member or other person who resides with a library patron and who is picking up the material on behalf of the patron" or a patron "may request that reserved materials be released only to the patron." MINN. STAT. § 13.40 (2007).

MISSISSIPPI

Mississippi state law provides that "[r]ecords maintained by any library funded in whole or in part by public funds, which contain information relating to the identity of a library user, relative to the user's use of books or other materials at the library, shall be confidential." The statute provides that "[s]uch records may only be released with the express written permission of the respective library user or as the result of a court order." MISS. CODE ANN. § 39-3-365 (2008).

MISSOURI

Missouri state law provides that "[n]otwithstanding the provisions of any other law to the contrary, no library or employee or agent of a library shall be required to release or disclose a library record or portion of a library record to any person or persons except: (1) in response to a written request of the person identified in that record, according to procedures and forms giving written consent as determined by the library; or (2) in response to an order issued by a court of competent jurisdiction upon a finding that the disclosure of such record is necessary to protect the public safety or to prosecute a crime." MO. STAT. § 182.817 (2008).

MONTANA

The Montana state legislature has mandated that "[n]o person may release or disclose a library record or portion of a library record to any person except in response to: (a) a written request of the person identified in that record, according to procedures and forms giving written consent as determined by the library; or (b) an order issued by a court of competent jurisdiction, upon a finding that the disclosure of such record is necessary because the merits of public disclosure clearly exceed the demand for individual privacy." The statute provides further that any person who improperly discloses a library record "is guilty of a misdemeanor and is liable to the person identified in a record that is improperly released or disclosed." The statute provides that the person whose record was disclosed improperly "may bring a civil action for actual damages or $100, whichever is greater," and that "[r]easonable attorney fees and the costs of bringing the action may be awarded to the prevailing party." MONT. CODE ANN. §§ 22-1-1103, 22-1-1111 (2007).

NEBRASKA

Nebraska state law provides that "[r]ecords or portions of records kept by a publicly funded library which, when examined with or without other records, reveal the identity of any library patron using the library's materials or services" may not be released "unless publicly disclosed in an open court, open administrative proceeding, or open meeting or disclosed by a public entity pursuant to its duties." NEB. REV. STAT. § 84-712.05(11) (2007).

NEVADA

The Nevada state legislature has mandated that "[a]ny records of a public library or other library which contain the identity of a user and the books, documents, films, recordings or other property of the library which he used are confidential" and that such public library records "may be disclosed only in response to an order issued by a court upon a finding that the disclosure of such records is necessary to protect the public safety or to prosecute a crime." NEV. REV. STAT. ANN. § 239.013 (2007).

NEW HAMPSHIRE

New Hampshire law provides that "library user" and "videotape sale or rental" records are exempt from disclosure because release of such materials would constitute an "invasion of privacy" (N.H. REV. STAT. ANN. § 91-A:5 [2008]). New Hampshire law also provides explicitly that, with limited exceptions, "[l]ibrary records which contain the names or other personal identifying information regarding the users of public or other than public libraries shall be confidential and shall not be disclosed." Library records may be disclosed only "to the extent necessary for the proper operation of such libraries and shall be disclosed upon request by or consent of the user or pursuant to subpoena, court order, or where otherwise required by statute" (N.H. REV. STAT. ANN. § 201-D:11 [2008]).

NEW JERSEY

The New Jersey state legislature has mandated that, with limited exceptions, "[l]ibrary records which contain the names or other personally identifying details regarding the users of libraries are confidential and shall not be disclosed." Disclosure is permitted only if (a) the records are necessary for the proper operation of the library; (b) disclosure is requested by the user; or (c) disclosure is required pursuant to a subpoena issued by a court or court order. N.J.S.A. § 18A:73-43.2 (2008).

NEW MEXICO

New Mexico state law provides that the purpose of protecting library records from public disclosure is to preserve "intellectual freedom . . . by providing privacy for users of the public libraries of the state with respect to the library materials that they wish to use." Thus, the statute provides that "[p]atron records shall not be disclosed or released to any person not a member of the library staff in the performance of his duties, except upon written consent of the person identified in the record, or except upon court order issued to the library." The statute provides further that the library "shall have the right to be represented by counsel at any hearing on disclosure or release of its patron records." The legislature further has mandated that any person who improperly releases library records "shall be subject to civil liability to the person identified in the released records for damages and costs of the action as determined by the court." N.M. STAT. ANN. §§ 18-9-2, 18-9-4, 18-9-6 (2008).

NEW YORK

The New York legislature has mandated that "[l]ibrary records, which contain names or other personally identifying details regarding the users of public, free association, school, college and university libraries and library systems of this state, including but not limited to records related to the circulation of library materials, computer database searches, interlibrary loan transactions, reference queries, requests for photocopies of library materials, title reserve requests, or the use of audio-visual materials, films or records, shall be confidential and shall not be disclosed except that such records may be disclosed to the extent necessary for the proper operation of such library and shall be disclosed upon request or consent of the user or pursuant to subpoena, court order or where otherwise required by statute." N.Y.C.P.L.R. § 4509 (2007).

NORTH CAROLINA

North Carolina law provides that "[a] library shall not disclose any library record that identifies a person as having requested or obtained specific materials, information, or services, or as otherwise having used the library" unless "necessary for the reasonable operation of the library," the patron has provided written consent, or the request is "[p]ursuant to subpoena, court order, or where otherwise required by law." N.C.G.S.A. § 125-19 (2008).

NORTH DAKOTA

The North Dakota state legislature has mandated that "[a]ny record maintained or received by a library receiving public funds, which provides a library patron's name or information sufficient to identify a patron together with the subject about which the patron requested information, is considered private and is excepted from the public records disclosure requirements." Library patron records may be released only "when required pursuant to a court order or a subpoena." N.D.C.C. ANN. § 40-38-12 (2008).

OHIO

Ohio state law provides that "[a] library shall not release any library record or disclose any patron information" except in the following limited circumstances: (1) "record or patron information pertaining to a minor child" if requested by the parent, guardian, or custodian; (2) pursuant to a subpoena, search warrant, or other court order; (3) to a law enforcement officer "acting in the scope of the officer's law enforcement duties and who is investigating a matter involving public safety in exigent circumstances"; (4) with the consent of the patron whose records have been requested; (5) "for administrative library purposes, including establishment or maintenance of a system to manage the library records or to assist in the transfer of library records from one records management system to another, compilation of statistical data on library use, and collection of fines and penalties"; and (6) documentation of "improper use of the internet at the library so long as any patron information is removed from those records." OHIO REV. CODE ANN. § 149.432 (2008).

OKLAHOMA

Oklahoma state law provides that "[a]ny library which is in whole or in part supported by public funds including but not limited to public, academic, school or special libraries, and having records indicating which of its documents or other materials, regardless of format, have been loaned to or used by an identifiable individual or group shall not disclose such records to any person," with limited exceptions. Library records may only be disclosed to (1) library administrators acting within the scope of their duties; (2) persons with written authorization from the patron to view the materials; and (3) pursuant to court order. 65 OKLA. STAT. § 1-05 (2008).

OREGON

The Oregon state legislature has mandated that "[t]he records of a library, including circulation records, showing use of specific library material by a named person or consisting of the name of a library patron together with the address or telephone number, or both, of the patron" are exempt from disclosure. OR. REV. STAT. § 192.502(23) (2007).

PENNSYLVANIA

Pennsylvania state law provides that "[r]ecords related to the circulation of library materials which contain the names or other personally identifying details regarding the users of the State Library or any local library which is established or maintained under any law of the Commonwealth or the library of any university, college or educational institution chartered by the Commonwealth or the library of any public school or branch reading room, deposit station or agency operated in connection therewith, shall be confidential and shall not be made available to anyone except by a court order in a criminal proceeding." 24 P.S. § 4428 (2008).

RHODE ISLAND

The Rhode Island state legislature has mandated that "[i]t is unlawful for any person to reveal, transmit, publish, or disseminate in any manner, any records which would identify the names and addresses of individuals, with the titles or nature of video films, records, cassettes, or the like, which they purchased, leased, rented, or borrowed, from libraries, book stores, video stores, or record and cassette shops or any retailer or distributor of those products, whether or not the identities and listings are kept in a remote computing service or electronic storage or the disclosure is made through or by a remote computing service," but that it "is not unlawful to make disclosures to other employees of the library or business that are incident to the normal course of their work or pursuant to lawful compulsion." The statute provides further that records of such transactions "shall be maintained as confidential and may only be released by written waiver" and that any person or entity that violates these provisions "shall be punished for each violation by a fine of not more than one thousand dollars ($1,000), by imprisonment for not more than six (6) months, or both." Moreover, the statute provides that "[a]ny person injured as a result of a violation of this section for each violation may bring a civil action against the violator for actual damages or for two hundred fifty dollars ($250), whichever is greater, plus reasonable attorneys' fees and court costs." R.I. GEN. LAWS § 11-18-32 (2008).

SOUTH CAROLINA

South Carolina law provides that "[r]ecords related to registration and circulation of library materials which contain names or other personally identifying details regarding the users of public, private, school, college, technical college, university, and state institutional libraries and library systems, supported in whole or in part by public funds or expending public funds, are confidential information." The statute provides further that "[r]ecords which by themselves or when examined with other public records would reveal the identity of the library patron checking out or requesting an item from the library or using other library services are confidential information." Additionally, the statute provides that the "confidential records may not be disclosed except to persons acting within the scope of their duties in the administration of the library or library system or persons authorized by the library patron to inspect his records, or in accordance with proper judicial order upon a finding that the disclosure of the records is necessary to protect public safety, to prosecute a crime, or upon showing of good cause before the presiding Judge in a civil matter." The statute provides further that any person convicted of violating these provisions "must upon conviction be fined not more than five hundred dollars or imprisoned for not more than thirty days for the first offense, must be fined not more than one thousand dollars or imprisoned for not more than sixty days for the second offense, and must be fined not more than two thousand dollars or imprisoned for not more than ninety days for the third or subsequent offense." S.C. CODE ANN. §§ 60-4-10, 60-4-30 (2007).

SOUTH DAKOTA

South Dakota state law provides that "[a]ll public library records containing personally identifiable information are confidential." Moreover, the statute provides that "[a]ny information contained in public library records may not be released except by court order or upon request of a parent of a child who is under eighteen years of age," and "personally identifiable" means "any information a library maintains that would identify a patron." S.D.C.L. § 14-2-51 (2008).

TENNESSEE

The Tennessee state legislature has mandated that, with limited exceptions, "no employee of a library shall disclose any library record that identifies a person as having requested or obtained specific materials, information, or services or as having otherwise used such library." Library records may be disclosed only in the following instances: (1) with written consent of the patron; (2) pursuant to a court order; or (3) when "used to seek reimbursement for or the return of lost, stolen, misplaced or otherwise overdue library materials." TENN. CODE ANN. § 10-8-102 (2008).

TEXAS

The Texas state legislature has mandated that "[a] record of a library or library system, supported in whole or in part by public funds, that identifies or serves to identify a person who requested, obtained, or used a library material or service" is exempt from disclosure, with limited exceptions. Library records may be disclosed where "reasonably necessary for the operation of the library or library system and the record is not confidential under other state or federal law." Library records may also be disclosed to a law enforcement officer or prosecutor pursuant to a "court order or subpoena obtained after a showing to a district court that: (A) disclosure of the record is necessary to protect the public safety; or (B) the record is evidence of an offense or constitutes evidence that a particular person committed an offense." V.T.C.A. § 552.124 (2007).

UTAH

Utah law provides that "records of publicly funded libraries that when examined alone or with other records identify a patron" are considered "private." Private records may only be disclosed in limited circumstances, including to the patron, to the parent or guardian of a minor, the guardian of a legally incapacitated individual, any individual who has power of attorney from the patron, or pursuant to court order. A court order may be relied upon to release library records only if "(a) the record deals with a matter in controversy over which the court has jurisdiction; (b) the court has considered the merits of the request for access to the record; and (c) the court has considered and, where appropriate, limited the requester's use and further disclosure of the record in order to protect privacy interests in the case of private or controlled records, business confidentiality interests in the case of records . . . and privacy interests or the public interest in the case of other protected records; (d) to the extent the record is properly classified private, controlled, or protected, the interests favoring access, considering limitations thereon, outweigh the interests favoring restriction of access; and (e) where access is restricted by a rule, statute, or regulation referred to in Subsection 63-2-201(3)(b), the court has authority independent of this chapter to order disclosure." UTAH CODE ANN. §§ 63G-2-202, 63G-2-302 (2008).

VERMONT

The Vermont legislature has mandated that "records relating to the identity of library patrons or the identity of library patrons in regard to the circulation of library materials" are exempt from public disclosure and copying. VT. STAT. ANN., tit. 1, § 317(c)(19) (2007).

VIRGINIA

Virginia state law provides that certain records are exempt from disclosure "but may be disclosed by the custodian in his discretion, except where such disclosure is prohibited by law." That statute encompasses "[l]ibrary records that can be used to identify both (i) any library patron who has borrowed material from a library and (ii) the material such patron borrowed." VA. CODE ANN. § 2.2-3705.7(3) (2008).

WASHINGTON

Washington state law provides that certain records are exempt from public disclosure and copying, including "[a]ny library record, the primary purpose of which is to maintain control of library materials, or to gain access to information, which discloses or could be used to disclose the identity of a library user." WASH. REV. CODE ANN. § 42.56.310 (2008).

WEST VIRGINIA

The West Virginia state legislature has mandated that "[c]irculation and similar records of any public library in this state which identify the user of library materials are not public records but shall be confidential and may not be disclosed" except in limited circumstances, including (1) to library staff in the ordinary course of business; (2) with written consent of the user of the library materials or the user's parents or guardian if the user is a minor or ward; or (3) pursuant to an appropriate court order or subpoena. W.VA. CODE ANN. § 10-1-22 (2008).

WISCONSIN

The Wisconsin state legislature has mandated that "[r]ecords of any library which is in whole or in part supported by public funds, including the records of a public library system, indicating the identity of any individual who borrows or uses the library's documents or other materials, resources, or services may not be disclosed" except in limited circumstances. Such records may be disclosed in the following instances: (1) pursuant to court order, (2) to other libraries for inter-library loan purposes provided certain statutory criteria are met, (3) to custodial parents or guardians of minors under the age of 16, and (4) to a law enforcement officer "who is investigating criminal conduct alleged to have occurred at a library," including "all records pertinent to the alleged criminal conduct that were produced by a surveillance device under the control of the library." WIS. STAT. § 43.30 (2008).

WYOMING

Wyoming state law provides that the custodian of records must deny inspection of records that are "[l]ibrary circulation and registration records except as required for administration of the library or except as requested by a custodial parent or guardian to inspect the records of his minor child." WYO. STAT. § 16-4-203 (2006).

Index

You may also be interested in

The Library Security and Safety Guide: Security planning, part of disaster response and continuous operations planning, is the key to proactively addressing potential safety issues. Look over the shoulder of disaster expert Kahn as she walks through key safety and security issues step by step, outlining potential security problems, the implementation of prevention strategies, guidelines for libraries and staff in case something does happen, and much more.

The Quality Library: Based on more than 50 years of author expertise in organizational improvement, this book offers a methodology pinpointing trouble areas in your library and improving processes. By developing a customer-focused system outlining library processes and networks, administrators and managers can quickly determine areas for improvement that apply directly to the library's goals and mission. Staff will also learn how to statistically document the performance of new processes, giving the library a means to quantify their effects.

Measuring Your Library's Value: This hands-on reference covers the economic basics of cost-benefit analysis (CBA) with librarian-friendly terms and examples, preparing library leaders to collaborate with economist-consultants. Authored by members of the team that developed, tested, and perfected this methodology over a decade, *Measuring Your Library's Value* is based on research funded by IMLS and PLA. Now you can credibly measure the dollars-and-cents value your library provides to your community.

Fundamentals of Library Supervision: Library managers and supervisors face staffing decisions every day. When priorities change quickly—whether relating to diversity, legal challenges, new technology, or simply a desire to build an exciting team and bring people together to do their best—it takes more than good intentions to achieve results. Two experienced library managers explain how to create a productive workplace as they weave practical advice and expert commentary into this easy-to-use resource.

For more information, please visit www.alastore.ala.org.